EVALUATING VIEWPOINTS:
CRITICAL THINKING IN UNITED STATES HISTORY SERIES

BOOK ONE
COLONIES
TO
CONSTITUTION

KEVIN O'REILLY

SERIES TITLES:
BOOK 1–COLONIES TO CONSTITUTION
BOOK 2–NEW REPUBLIC TO CIVIL WAR
BOOK 3–RECONSTRUCTION TO PROGRESSIVISM
BOOK 4–SPANISH-AMERICAN WAR TO VIETNAM WAR

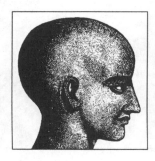

© 1983, 1990
CRITICAL THINKING BOOKS & SOFTWARE
(FORMERLY MIDWEST PUBLICATIONS)
WWW.CRITICALTHINKING.COM
PHONE 800-458-4849 • FAX 831-393-3277
ISBN 0-89455-413-1
PRINTED IN THE UNITED STATES OF AMERICA

ABOUT THE AUTHOR

Kevin O'Reilly is a social studies teacher at Hamilton-Wenham Regional High School in Massachusetts. He was named by *Time* magazine and the National Council for the Social Studies as the 1986 Outstanding Social Studies Teacher in the United States. In addition to these four volumes on Critical Thinking in United States History, Mr. O'Reilly is the coauthor of *Critical Viewing: Stimulant to Critical Thinking* (also published by Midwest Publications/Critical Thinking Press & Software) and the author of "Escalation," the computer simulation on the Vietnam War (Kevin O'Reilly, 6 Mason Street, Beverly, MA 01915). Mr. O'Reilly, who has a Master of Arts Degree in History, is an editor of the *New England Journal of History*. He conducts workshops throughout the United States on critical thinking, critical viewing, and decision making.

ACKNOWLEDGEMENTS

I would like to thank Richard Trask of the Danvers Archival Center for his suggestions on the Salem Witch Trials (Lesson 10); Bob Swartz of the University of Massachusetts at Boston for his ideas on teaching specific thinking skills, especially cause and effect and generalization; William Payne, a history teacher at Moreno Valley High School in California, for his questions to test value claims; Dick Aieta, Vincent Bucci, Vicki Krupp, Ken Portnoy, Alice Schlossberg, and Ann Tassanari of the social studies department at Hamilton-Wenham for their ideas and support—we've shared and tried out a lot of ideas for teaching history; and my wife Lynn for her love, patience, and support.

— *Kevin O'Reilly*

TABLE OF CONTENTS

INTRODUCTION

Thinking is what history is all about, as we try to more fully understand our past and thereby ourselves. We don't have many answers in history. Instead, we search for the truth, always attempting to get closer to what really happened. This book is meant to give you a taste of the excitement of historical interpretation and debate. It is also meant to give you guidance in learning the skills necessary to evaluate conflicting viewpoints. The goal is to empower you, as citizens in a democratic society, to make decisions for yourself regarding what you read, see, or hear about the issues of tomorrow—issues where there are few easy answers, and where reasonable people disagree.

This book is about historical interpretations or viewpoints. It is not itself a history book, but rather a series of problems on which historians present differing opinions. The purpose of the book is to teach you how to analyze and evaluate historical arguments.

If you think of a social, political, or economic issue today, you'll realize that people approach problems with different viewpoints. For example, reasonable people disagree about how much money should be spent on social welfare programs, about how to fight crime, and about the best candidate in an election. Historians also disagree about many events in history. Just as there are different ways to tell a fictional story, so there are many ways to tell the story of history. Historians, depending upon their backgrounds and frames of reference, select different information as important or unimportant.

The root word of history is story. As a "story," history seeks to explain past events. Why did a particular event happen when it did? How did a particular person or group of people affect the world around them? What underlying forces shaped events? Good historians have taken the time to step back, to carefully examine events to see the whole picture more clearly, to explain events more fully, and, thereby, to help our understanding of the world.

There are two broad kinds of history: analytical and narrative. In analytical history a historian makes a strong argument about an issue. The thesis is obvious, and the rest of the interpretation consists of a series of arguments to support the thesis. You probably have written thesis/support arguments in your English or social studies classes.

The second kind of history is narrative. Here, the historian tells a story, usually in chronological order. The various elements of the situation—economic forces, technological changes, social institutions, personalities, and so forth—are brought together as the drama unfolds. The main argument or thesis is not always obvious in narrative history. It has to be inferred from the way the story is told. Nevertheless, narrative history also contains a point of view or a thesis about why events happened the way they did.

This book presents both analytical and narrative history. For example, several interpretations on the Salem Witch Trials (Lesson 10) are narrative; others are analytical; most are a combination of both.

One of the most important goals of this book is to introduce you to the conflicting viewpoints or interpretations of history. Ideally, you would read various historical interpretations of events, some of which are listed on pages 129–130. Realistically, you don't have the time to read all of these historical works. So this book contains short summaries of the interpretations. In some cases 300-page books have been summarized into one or two pages. Since this isn't fair to the original historians, their names have been replaced by titles: Historian A, Historian B, and so forth.

In some lessons the viewpoints are entitled Interpretation A or Theory A, rather than Historian A. Interpretation or Theory is used when no particular historian is identified with that point of view. These terms are also used to convey the idea that you should be forming your own interpretations or theories. The dictionary defines interpretation as "an explanation of what is not immediately plain or obvious," and it defines theory as "a judgment based on evidence or analysis." Ask your science teacher how the term *theory* is defined in science.

While most arguments presented in this book are those expressed by historians, a few are from historical participants. Thus, there are arguments by British and Colonial leaders on the Revolution (Lesson 16) and by James Madison and an Antifederalist on the Constitution (Lessons 23 and 24).

This student book is comprised of three components:
Guide to Critical Thinking explains the parts of an argument and how to evaluate those parts.
Worksheets provide practice in the skills necessary for evaluating and constructing arguments.
Historical interpretation problems provide the opportunity for you to analyze historical arguments and make up your own mind.

Lessons within the book are arranged into three units: Colonies (Lessons 1–10), American Revolution (Lessons 11–19), and Constitution (Lessons 20–29). Thirteen of the lessons (#1–6, 11–14, 19, 22, and 28) are short worksheet lessons which focus on practicing particular skills. The other sixteen lessons (#7–10, 15–18, 20, 21, 22–27, and 29) are longer problems where the skills can be applied.

© 1990 MIDWEST PUBLICATIONS, P.O. Box 448, Pacific Grove, CA 93950

Purpose of This Unit

This Guide is meant to help you improve your critical thinking skills. Critical Thinking, as used in this book, means evaluating or judging arguments. The critical thinker asks, "Why should I believe this?" or "How do I know this is true?" Just as importantly, critical thinking means constructing good arguments. Here, the critical thinker asks, "Why do I believe this?" and "Do I have a logical, well-supported case to back up my claims?"

As mentioned in the Introduction to this text, you are going to be confronted in this book with opposing viewpoints. You will have to decide for yourself which are stronger and which are weaker. This Guide will help you with the critical thinking skills necessary to judge the viewpoints presented and to express your own verbal and written views on topics.

Historians use critical thinking skills constantly in evaluating the reliability of documents, in selecting what is important, and in determining the underlying causes for events. But critical thinking is useful in everyday life as well. It is called for in such situations as buying a car, watching the news, voting, or deciding on a job or career. Improved skills in this area will help you make better judgments more often.

You can get an overall picture of critical thinking by reading through this Guide. You will find it most useful, however, when you need to use a particular skill in a particular lesson. For example, the section on evaluating generalizations will be useful in Lesson 9, which asks several questions on recognizing and drawing good generalizations.

When Is an Argument Not a Fight?

An *argument* or interpretation, as used in this Guide, refers to presenting a conclusion and defending it with reasons that logically lead to the conclusion. You will have to decide for yourself how strong each argument is. A *case* is a set of arguments. The strength of a case may be judged by examining individual arguments. Arguments or interpretations may include any or all of the following components.

• Assertions • Evidence • Reasoning •
• Assumptions • Values •

Keep the importance of words in mind as you look through the following pages. Words are the keys to arguments. Signal words like "but," "however," and "on the other hand" indicate a change of direction in an argument. Words will serve as your clues in identifying parts of an argument and, once the argument has been identified, they will serve as your keys in analyzing the strength of that argument.

Once you recognize an argument, you will want to analyze it. You will break it down into its respective parts and evaluate the elements against certain standards of excellence in reasoning and evidence. You will examine the assumptions to see if they are warranted. You will consider how the author's values shape the evidence and reasoning presented.

Assertions

An assertion is a statement, conclusion, main point, or claim concerning an issue, person, or idea. It can be the conclusion of a very short argument, or it can be the main point (thesis) of an argument of perhaps two or more paragraphs.

For example, consider the short argument, "Bob is very responsible, so I'm sure he'll show up." The conclusion (assertion) in the argument is the phrase "...so I'm sure he'll show up." (The part of the argument that isn't the conclusion ["Bob is very responsible,...] is called the premise. Premises are assumptions or reasons offered to support a conclusion. See the section on Assumptions, pages 15–16.)

IDENTIFYING ASSERTIONS

Words that often cue an assertion or conclusion include "therefore," "then," "so," and "thus." You can also identify an assertion by asking yourself, "What is the author trying to prove? Of what is the author trying to convince me?"

EVALUATING ASSERTIONS

Two important questions to ask to evaluate the overall assertion of an argument are:

- Is the assertion supported by good reasons (supporting arguments)?
- Are the reasons supported by evidence?

Evidence

Evidence consists of the information a person uses to support assertions. It is the data, information, and knowledge which a historian, social scientist, or any communicator uses to support an argument; it is not the argument or interpretation itself.

There are many sources of evidence. Some of the more common sources include statements by witnesses or other people, written documents, objects, photographs, and video recordings. Lack of sources for evidence seriously weakens an argument. That is why many historical works include footnotes to cite sources; that is also why you should cite sources in essays you write.

For example, historians studying a Civil War battle could gather written accounts of the battle from sources such as diaries, battle reports, and letters. They could examine objects that had been found on the battlefield and photographs taken at the time of the battle. They also might use accounts by other historians, but these would be weaker sources because they are not eyewitness accounts (see primary sources below).

IDENTIFYING EVIDENCE

To help locate evidence in an argument, look for endnotes, quotation marks, or such words as "according to," "so-and-so said," or "such-and-such shows."

The initial questions to be asked when evaluating any evidence offered in support of an argument should be:
- Is there a source given for this information?
- If so, what is it?

EVALUATING EVIDENCE

Only when you know the sources of evidence can you judge how reliable the evidence actually is. Frequently, you can use the following evaluation method when considering evidence and its sources. This can be shortened to **PROP**; remind students that good sources will "prop up" evidence.

P Is it a primary (eyewitness) or secondary (not an eyewitness) source?

Primary sources are invariably more desirable. To reach valid conclusions, you need to realize the importance of primary sources and gather as many as possible to use as evidence in an argument. You should depend on secondary sources, like encyclopedias or history texts, only when primary are unavailable.

R If the source is a person, does he or she have any reason to distort the evidence?

Would those giving the statement, writing the document, recording the audio (or video), or identifying the object benefit if the truth were distorted, covered up, falsified, sensationalized, or manipulated? Witnesses with no reason to distort the evidence are more desirable than those who might benefit from a particular presentation of the evidence.

O Are there other witnesses, statements, recordings, or evidence which report the same data, information, or knowledge?

Having other evidence verify the initial evidence strengthens the argument.

P Is it a public or private statement?

If the person making the statement of evidence knew or intended that other people should hear it, then it is a public statement. A private statement may be judged more accurate because it was probably said in confidence and is, therefore, more likely to reflect the speaker's true feelings or observations.

These four factors (**PROP**) will be enough to evaluate most evidence you encounter. Additional factors that are sometimes considered regarding evidence include:

Witnesses

- What are the frames of reference (points of view) of the witnesses? What are their values? What are their backgrounds?
- Are the witnesses expert (recognized authorities) on what they saw?
- Did the witnesses believe their statements could be checked? (If I believe you can check my story with other witnesses, I am more likely to tell the truth.)
- Was what the witnesses said an observation ("Maria smiled.") or an inference ("Maria was happy.")? Inferences are judgments that can reveal much about the witnesses' points of view or motives (reasons) for making statements.

Observation Conditions

- Were physical conditions conducive to witnessing the event? (Was it foggy? Noisy? Dark?)
- What was the physical location of the witnesses in relation to the event? Were they close to the action? Was there anything blocking their view?

Witnesses' Statement or Document

- Is the document authentic or a forgery?
- What is the reputation of the source containing the document?
- How soon after the event was the statement made?
- Did the witnesses use precise techniques or tools to report or record the event? For example, did they take notes or use reference points?

Reasoning

Just as evidence can be judged for its reliability, so reasoning can be evaluated for its logic.

Reasoning is the logical process through which a person reaches conclusions. For example, you notice that the car is in the driveway (evidence) so you reason that your mother is home (conclusion). Five kinds of reasoning are frequently used in historical interpretations.

- cause and effect
- comparison
- generalization
- proof (by evidence, example, or authority)
- debating (eliminating alternatives).

These types of reasoning, along with questions to help evaluate them and fallacies (errors in reasoning) for each, are explained below.

Reasoning by Cause and Effect

This type of reasoning is used when someone argues that something caused, brought about, or will result in something else. For example, Laura's motorcycle will not start (effect), so she decides it must be out of gas (proposed cause).

Causation is very complex—so complex that some historians feel that they don't really understand the causes of an event even after years of study. Other historians don't even use the word cause; instead they talk about change. Please keep a sense of humility when you study causation. When you finish your course, you aren't going to know all the causes of complex events. Rather, you're going to know a little bit more about how to sort out causes.

Historians believe in multiple causation, that is, that every event has several or many causes. This belief does not, however, relieve us of the responsibility of trying to figure out which are the most important causes. Indeed, one of the most frequent sources of debate among historians stems from disagreements over the main causes of events.

IDENTIFYING CAUSE-AND-EFFECT REASONING

One way to identify cause and effect reasoning is to watch for such cue words as "caused," "led to," "forced," "because," "brought about," "resulted in," or "reason for." You can also identify it by asking, "Is the author arguing that one thing resulted from another?"

EVALUATING CAUSE-AND-EFFECT REASONING

Several important questions may be used to evaluate the strength of a causal explanation.

- Is there a **reasonable connection** between the cause and the effect? Does the arguer state the connection?

  In the motorcycle example, for instance, there is a reasonable connection between the motorcycle being out of gas and not starting. Lack of gasoline would cause a motorcycle not to start.

- Might there be **other possible causes** for this effect? Has the arguer eliminated these as possible causes?

  There are also, however, other possible causes for a motorcycle failing to start. Maybe the starter isn't working. Other possible causes have not been eliminated.

- Might there be **important previous causes** that led to the proposed cause?

  In some cases a previous cause might be more important than the proposed cause; e.g., a leak in the gasoline tank might cause a motorcycle to be out of gasoline. In this case simply putting gasoline in the tank will not make the engine run again.

Cause-and-Effect Fallacies

Single cause

Any conclusion that a historical event had but one cause commits the single-cause fallacy. For example, the statements "Eloise married Jon because he's handsome" and "Antiwar protest caused the United States to pull out of the Vietnam War" both make use of the single-cause fallacy.

In both cases there are likely to be other factors, or causes, involved. The fallacy can be avoided by carefully investigating and explaining the complexity of causes. Be careful, however. Historians may sometimes assert that something "caused" an event when they really mean it was the main, not the only, cause.

Preceding event as cause

A Latin phrase (*Post hoc, ergo propter hoc*), meaning "after this, therefore because of this," is the technical name of a fallacy that occurs when someone assumes that because event B happened after event A, A caused B. "I washed my car, so naturally it rained" and "Since the Depression followed the stock market crash of 1929, the stock market crash must have caused it" are both examples of this fallacy. To avoid the error, the author of the argument must explain how A caused B.

Correlation as cause

This fallacy occurs when a conclusion is reached that because A and B occurred at the same time or occur regularly at the same time (the correlation), then one caused the other.

Some correlations, such as cigarette smoking and increased incidence of heart disease, are very strong. Others are not as strong. In some correlations where A is argued to cause B, ask yourself if B could instead have caused A. For example, "Students who have fewer absences (A) achieve higher grades in school (B)." In this case, consideration might also be given to the correlation that "Students who achieve higher grades in school (B) have fewer absences (A)."

Again, the fallacy might be avoided by an explanation of how A caused B. Since, however, a connection cannot always be shown, people are frequently forced to rely on correlations. For example, you don't have to know, mechanically, *how* a car works to know that turning the ignition should cause it to start.

False scenario

This fallacy uses the argument that if something had happened, then something else would have happened (or if something had not happened, then something else would not have happened). "If you hadn't told Mother on me, I wouldn't be in trouble" is an example of false-scenario reasoning. "If we had not built railroads in the late 1800s, the United States would not have had as much economic growth as it did with the railroads" is another.

© 1990 *MIDWEST PUBLICATIONS*, P.O. Box 448, Pacific Grove, CA 93950

Although some of this kind of predicting can occur when we have a great deal of evidence regarding what might have happened, it is generally much less certain than causal reasoning about what actually did happen. To avoid this fallacy, concern yourself with what actually happened rather than what might have happened.

Reasoning by Comparison

This type of reasoning, sometimes called "reasoning by analogy," involves drawing comparisons between two cases and includes two basic types.

Alike comparison

The first type of comparison chooses two cases (people, events, objects, etc.) and reasons that since they are alike in some ways, they will be alike in some other way. For example, Joe might reason that Fernandez did all his homework and got an "A" in geometry, so if Joe does all of his homework he can also get an "A." Joe is reasoning that since the two cases (his and Fernandez's) are similar in terms of homework (doing it all), they will be similar in terms of outcome (an "A").

Difference comparison

The second type compares two cases and reasons that since they are different in some respect, something must be true. For example, Juan might reason that his baseball team is better than Cleon's, since Juan's team won more games. Juan is concluding that since the two cases (teams) are different in some respect (one team won more games than the other), it is true that the team that won the most games is a better team.

In comparison reasoning, the more similarities the two cases share, the stronger the comparison. If Joe and Fernandez are taking the same course (geometry), and have the same mathematical ability and the same teacher, then the conclusion that the outcome would be the same is stronger than it would be if they were different in any or all these areas. If the two baseball teams played the same opponents and the same number of games, then the conclusion that one team is better (different) than the other is stronger than it would be if they were different in any of these ways.

However, if the two baseball teams had the same winning percentage, then the conclusion that one was better (different) than the other would be weakened by this similarity. As another example of a difference comparison, examine the argument: "The federal budget deficit increased from $800 billion three years ago to $912 billion this year. We've got to do something about it before it destroys our economy." What if the federal budget deficit were 4% of the Gross National Product (the measure of goods and services produced in a year) three years ago and 4% this year also? Here, a similarity found between the deficits of the two years being compared weakens the conclusion that the federal budget deficit is getting worse. Thus, differences weaken arguments comparing similarities, and similarities weaken arguments comparing differences.

IDENTIFYING
COMPARISON
REASONING

Cue words can help identify comparisons. Watch for such comparative terms as "like," "similar to," "same as," "greater (or less) than," "better (or worse) than," and "increased (or decreased)." Some comparisons, however, are implied rather than stated. For example, someone might say, "Oh, I wouldn't travel by plane. It's too dangerous." You might ask "dangerous compared to what?" If a higher percentage of people are injured or killed using alternate methods of travel (automobiles, trains), then the statement is weakened considerably.

EVALUATING
COMPARISON
REASONING

> In examining comparisons, ask yourself:
> • How are the cases similar; how are they different?

Usually, more similarities make a stronger argument. A similarity found in an argument of difference, however, will weaken the argument. It is important to remember that this skill involves *evaluating comparison arguments*. It is not the same activity as "compare and contrast," where you are asked to find the similarities and differences between two items; i.e., "Compare and contrast the American and French Revolutions." In evaluating comparison arguments you, on your own, are to recognize that a comparison argument is being made and, without being told, ask about the similarities and differences of the two cases being compared.

**Reasoning by
Generalization**

This kind of reasoning includes both definitional and statistical generalizations. The generalization, "No U.S. senator is under 30 years of age" is an example of a *definitional generalization*, since by legal definition, a U.S. senator must be at least 30 years of age.

Statistical generalization is important to evaluating historical arguments. Statistical generalizations argue that what is true for some (part or sample) of a group (such as wars, women, or songs) will be true in roughly the same way for all of the group. For example, Maribeth might argue that since the bite of pizza she took (sample) is cold, the whole pizza (the whole group) is cold.

Statistical generalizations can be further subdivided into two types. *Hard generalizations* are those applied to all (or none) of the members of a group, e.g., the whole cold pizza above, or a statement like "All the apples have fallen off the tree." A hard generalization is disproved by one counterexample (contrary case). For example, if there is one apple still on the tree, the generalization is disproved.

© 1990 MIDWEST PUBLICATIONS, P.O. Box 448, Pacific Grove, CA 93950

Soft generalizations are those applied to most (or few) members of a group, e.g., "Most people remember the Vietnam War." A soft generalization is not disproved by one—or even several—contrary cases, but the generalization is weakened as the contrary cases add up. For example, if someone says that Luis doesn't remember the Vietnam War, the generalization is not disproved. If, however, that person cites fifty people who don't remember the Vietnam War, the generalization is getting shaky.

The probability that a statistical generalization is correct increases with the size of the sample and the degree to which a sample is representative of the whole group. Your generalization that "Nella is prompt" is more likely to be accurate if she was on time on all twenty occasions when she was supposed to meet you than if she was on time the only time she was supposed to meet you.

Representativeness is even more important than size in generalizations. In the pizza example the sample is quite small (only one bite from the whole pizza) but very representative—if one part of the pizza is cold, it is highly likely that the whole pizza is cold. Similarly, presidential election polls are small (about 1200 people polled) but usually very accurate, since those sampled are quite representative of the whole electorate. If you think of the whole group of voters as a circle, a presidential election poll might look like Figure 1.

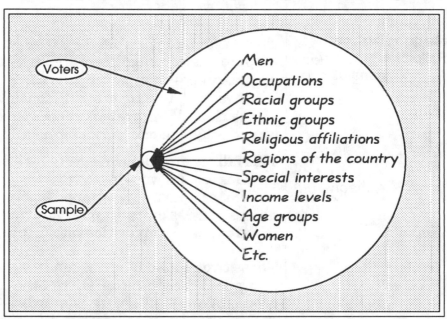

Figure 1. The sample should represent all groups of voters (and many more) in the same proportion as they make up the whole electorate.

IDENTIFYING GENERALIZATIONS

You can recognize statistical generalizations by watching for their cue words: "all," "none," "some," "most," "a majority," "few" or plural nouns ("women," "farmers," or "people").

EVALUATING
GENERALIZATIONS

Questions you should ask when evaluating generalizations include the following.

> - How large is the sample?
>   The strength of a statistical generalization is improved by larger sized sampling.
> - How representative is the sample?
>   If you picture the generalization as a little circle and a big circle, as in Figure 1, the question becomes: Does the little circle have all the same subgroups in the same proportion as the big circle?

You should not, however, be concerned only with evaluating generalizations that other people make. You should also be concerned with how far you can legitimately generalize from what you know.

For example, if you learned that slaves on ten large cotton plantations in Maryland in the 1850s were brutally treated, you might generalize that slaves on most large cotton plantations in Maryland at that time were brutally treated. You would be on much shakier ground, however, to generalize that slaves on most plantations were brutally treated at all times. You really have no information about slaves on, say, small Virginia tobacco plantations in the 1720s, so you shouldn't make such a broad generalization. The warning is, "Do not overgeneralize."

Generalization Fallacies
Hasty generalization

This fallacy consists of a general conclusion based on an inappropriately small or unrepresentative sample. For example, suppose a reporter polls three people in Illinois, all of whom say they support gun control. If the reporter concludes that all (or even most) people in Illinois support gun control, then he or she is making a hasty generalization.

Composition and division (stereotyping)

This fallacy includes such oversimplifications as "If it weren't for bankers, we wouldn't have wars." To avoid such fallacies, remember that any group (such as people, wars, or depressions) is quite complex and must be carefully sampled to take those complexities into account.

These two related fallacies confuse the characteristics of the group and the characteristics of the individuals within that group. In composition, the characteristics of the individual(s) within the group are ascribed (given) to the whole group. ("She's a good lawyer, so the law firm she is a member of must be a good firm.") In division, characteristics that belong to the group as a whole are assumed to belong to each of the individuals. ("She's a member of a good law firm, so she must be a good lawyer.")

These fallacies are commonly referred to as *stereotyping*, which is defined as "applying preconceived ideas to a group or members of a group." This results in the groups or individuals being judged before we really know them. This act of prejudging is where we derive the word *prejudice*. "You're Jewish, so you must be well educated" and "Of course he's a drinker, he's Irish!" are examples of stereotype statements.

Special pleading

In this fallacy the arguer presents a conclusion based on information favorable to the argument while ignoring unfavorable information. ("Mom, I should be able to go to the dance. I passed my history test and got an 'A' in math." [...omitting the information that I failed science and English.]) A good argument avoids this fallacy by including unfavorable information and overcoming it with compelling reasons for accepting the thesis or conclusion.

Reasoning by Proof (evidence, example, or authority)

These types of reasoning concern whether or not the evidence or authority used supports the point being argued. It does not concern the strengths and weakness of the evidence itself (see the **Evidence** section of the Guide). Similarly, the word "proof" as used here does not mean absolute proof—as in mathematics—but rather refers to methods used to support an argument or interpretation.

This is generally a legitimate method of supporting an argument. For example, a doctor might be called to testify in court to support the argument that a claimant had certain injuries (proof by authority). A biologist might explain the results of several investigations (example), cite evidence gathered (evidence), and quote the written opinions of several experts (authority) to support an argument on the effects of toxic waste.

IDENTIFYING PROOF REASONING

Proof reasoning can be identified by cue words such as "for example," "for instance," "according to," "authority," and "expert." When evaluating argument by proof, you should look at the answers to several questions:

EVALUATING PROOF

Evidence

- Does the evidence prove the point being argued? Does it support the point under consideration?

Example

- Are the examples pertinent to the argument?

Authority

- Is this person an expert on this particular topic? What are the qualifications of the authority? Are they presented?

- Do other authorities agree with these conclusions? Are there any authorities who disagree with the conclusion? Are counterarguments acknowledged and/or refuted?

**Fallacies
of Proof**

*Irrelevant
proof*

Arguments which present compelling evidence that does not apply to the argument in question are fallacies of irrelevant proof. For example, "If you flunk me, I'll lose my scholarship" and "Everyone else does it" are fallacies of irrelevant proof. As a further example, suppose Senator Smith is accused of taking bribes to vote for certain laws and, in his defense, presents a great deal of evidence that shows he is a good family man. This evidence does not concern his actions as a senator and is thus irrelevant to the charges. Good arguments avoid this fallacy by sticking to the issue under question.

*Negative
proof*

This fallacy type presents a conclusion based on the lack or absence of evidence to the contrary. For example, "There is no evidence that Senator Macklem is an honest woman, so it's obvious she is a crook" or "Since you haven't proven that there is no Santa Claus, there must be one." Remember that you must present evidence to **support** your conclusions when you are making a case.

*Prevalent
proof*

Related to the fallacy of negative proof, this fallacy concludes that something must be the case because "everyone knows" it is the case. Such arguments as "Everyone knows she's a winner" and "Politicians can't be trusted; everyone knows that" are examples of the prevalent proof fallacy. Remember, in previous times "everyone knew" that the sun revolved around the earth! The critical thinker sometimes asks questions even about things which everyone knows.

Numbers

A conclusion that the argument is right solely because of the great amount of evidence gathered commits the fallacy of numbers. For example, "We checked hundreds of thousands of government records, so our theory must be right."

Notice that no mention is made of what the "government records" contained—the argument only states that they were "checked." A great deal of evidence can be amassed to support a slanted perspective or an argument using poor reasoning or faulty assumptions. When constructing arguments, check them not only for strong evidence but also for sound reasoning and assumptions.

*Appeal
to authority*

A conclusion that is based only on the statement of an expert commits the appeal-to-authority fallacy. Such arguments conclude, "I'm right because I'm an expert" and lack additional supporting evidence. For example, the argument "It must be true because it says so right here in the book" is based only on the "authority" of the book's author. Arguments must be judged on the strength of their evidence and their reasoning rather than solely on the authority of their authors.

© 1990 MIDWEST PUBLICATIONS, P.O. Box 448, Pacific Grove, CA 93950

Appeal to the golden mean

This logical fallacy is committed when the argument is made that the conclusion is right because it is moderate (between the extreme views). If someone argued, "Some people say Adolf Hitler was right in what he did, while others say he was one of the most evil leaders in history. These views are so extreme that a more moderate view must be right. He must have been an average leader," he or she would be appealing to the golden mean. (Of course, the "extreme" view that Hitler was evil is right in this case.)

This fallacy can be avoided by realizing that there is no necessary reason for an extreme view to be wrong simply because it is extreme. At one time it was considered "extreme" to think that women should vote or that people would fly.

Reasoning by Debate (eliminating alternatives)

Reasoning by debate helps a person see why one interpretation should be believed over other interpretations and puts an interpretation into a context. It is not surprising, therefore, that articles in historical journals frequently begin by a survey of other interpretations of the topic under study and an attempt to refute opposing interpretations.

This type of reasoning advances an argument by referring to and attempting to show the weaknesses of alternative interpretations. This attempt to disprove, called debating, is not only acceptable, but desirable. For example, someone might argue, "Peter thinks Mi-Ling will get the lead role in the play, but he's wrong. Lucetta has a better voice and more acting experience, so she'll get the lead." A historian might argue, "Although the traditional view is that slavery is the main cause of the Civil War, people who hold that view are wrong. Economic problems, especially over the tariff, were the main cause of the bloody war." Both are applying reasoning by debate.

IDENTIFYING DEBATES

Cue words for this type of reasoning include "other people believe," "the traditional view is," "other views are wrong because," "older interpretations," and "other viewpoints are."

EVALUATING DEBATES

To help evaluate debate reasoning, ask questions like the following.

> • Have all reasonable alternatives been considered? Have they all been eliminated as possibilities?
> • Does this author attack the other views in a fair way?
> • What might the authors of the other views say in response to this argument?

In eliminating possible alternatives, the author must be careful to attack the argument rather than the arguer, to present reasoned evidence against the argument, and to fairly interpret the alternative argument under consideration. This form of questioning can also be helpful when there is a lack of information.

Fallacies of Debate

Either-or

This fallacy presents a conclusion that since A and B were the only possible explanations—and since A was not possible, B is proven to be the explanation. For example, "Only Willis and Cross were around, but Willis was swimming so Cross must have done it." What if someone else was actually around but no one saw him or her?

Of course, eliminating alternative can be very important to reasoning a problem through, as Sherlock Holmes demonstrates so well. But one must be careful to ask: Have all alternatives been eliminated? Could it be both alternatives? Don't let yourself be "boxed in" by this type of reasoning.

Attacking the arguer

(In logical terminology, this is called *ad hominem*–Latin for "to the man.") This fallacy occurs when statements are directed at the person making the argument rather than at the arguments presented. For example, the statement "No one should listen to what Mrs. Rouge says. She's a Communist" is an attack on Mrs. Rouge personally rather than on the statement she made.

Sometimes the attack is more subtle, such as a look of disgust, a negative comment ("I don't believe you just said that"), or sarcastic laughter. Good arguments avoid this fallacy by refuting the argument, not the person.

"Straw man"

This is the technique of attacking the opponents' argument by adding to or changing what a person said, then attacking the additions or changes. For example, Johannas says he's opposed to capital punishment, and Thibedeau replies, "People like you who oppose punishing criminals make me sick." (Johannas didn't say he opposed punishing criminals.) When constructing an argument, remember to be fair and argue against what your opponents said, not your version of what they said.

There are many methods of trying to prove something. The types of reasoning explained above (cause and effect; comparisons; generalizations; proof by evidence, example, or authority; and debate) are all methods of proof to be considered when evaluating historical arguments. The next section examines assumptions, which are like reasoning in that they lead to conclusions (assertions). They are different from reasoning, however, in that they aren't always consciously argued. Authors frequently don't realize the assumptions they are making.

Assumptions

An assumption is the part of an argument containing the ideas or opinions that the arguer takes for granted. Stated assumptions are not of concern for the purposes of this Guide. When authors say they are assuming something, all you decide is whether you agree with the stated assumption.

GENERAL UNSTATED
ASSUMPTIONS

Unstated assumptions are more difficult to recognize. There are two types of unstated assumptions: the general, more encompassing type and the specific type.

These assumptions are part of the argument as a whole and, as such, cannot be identified by rewriting particular arguments. In any argument there are an infinite number of such assumptions. For example, if you say you are going to the store to buy a TV, you are making the general assumptions that the store will be there, that you won't die on the way, that they'll have televisions in stock, and so forth. Some assumptions are trivial or unlikely, but others are very important. For example, if the President of the United States says, "We will not agree to the Soviet proposal to have both countries eliminate half of their missiles because we cannot check on them adequately," he is assuming the Soviets cannot be trusted. If, on the other hand, the President agreed to missile reductions without a means of verifying Soviet reductions, he would then be assuming the Soviets can be trusted. He might or might not be right in either case. The important point is that we should recognize his assumption.

General assumptions shape historical interpretations. A historian who assumes that economics drives people's behavior will select economic information and write from that perspective; a historian who assumes that politics, in the form of power and compromise, shapes society will focus on that area in both research and writing.

SPECIFIC UNSTATED
ASSUMPTIONS

To understand specific unstated assumption you need to know something about the form of arguments. As was explained in the section on **Assertions**, arguments are made up of the conclusion and the rest of the argument, which is designed to prove the conclusion. The sentences that comprise the rest of the argument are called *premises*.

Short arguments take the form of *premise, premise, conclusion*. A well-known example is: "Socrates is a man. All men are mortal. Therefore, Socrates is mortal." In premise, premise, conclusion format, this would be:

Premise: Socrates is a man.

Premise: All men are mortal.

Conclusion: Therefore, Socrates is mortal.

If the above argument "looks funny," it's because people rarely talk this way. In normal speech, we often state the conclusion first: "I should be able to go outside now. My homework is done." It is also common to not state one of the premises or the conclusion at all. For example, if we are trying to decide who should pay for the broken vase, you might say, "Well, Joaquin pushed me into it." Your point (although you didn't state it) is that Joaquin should pay.

When you leave out a premise, you are making an assumption. For example, the argument "We should spend our vacation in the mountains because we need a rest," can be rewritten this way:

> *Premise:*   We need a rest.
>
> *Premise:*   ??
>
> *Conclusion:* (Therefore) we should spend our vacation in the mountains.

The missing premise is the assumption.

IDENTIFYING ASSUMPTIONS

You can figure out what the assumption is by asking, "What has to be true for this conclusion to be true?" In the above case, the missing premise (assumption) is: "The mountains are a good place to rest."

EVALUATING ASSUMPTIONS

When you have identified an assumption, evaluate it by asking if the assumption is correct. Assumptions are frequently related to the beliefs and values of the author, as explained in the next section.

Values

Values are conditions that the person making an argument believes are important, worthwhile, or intrinsically good for themselves, their family, their country, and their world. Money, success, friendship, love, health, peace, power, freedom, and equality are examples of things people may value.

It is often important to discover the underlying values of the author of an argument, since assumptions made by an author are often related to the author's beliefs and values. This will help you understand why the viewpoint is argued the way it is, and, in cases where your values may be different from the author's values, it will help you understand why you might disagree with the argument. For example, if you believe that peace is more important than demonstrating power, then you are going to disagree with an argument which says that since Country A increased its power by attacking Country B, it was right to attack.

IDENTIFYING VALUE STATEMENTS

Clues to an author's value judgments are found in sentences containing words such as "good," "bad," "right," "wrong," "justified," "should," or "should not." For example, if someone says "The U.S. was wrong (value judgment) to drop the atomic bomb on Hiroshima because so many people were killed," that person is saying that life (value) is more important than the other conditions or values involved (power, peace vs. war, etc.).

To help identify an author's values, ask:
- Who wrote this?
- What beliefs does this person hold?

When you have identified a value judgment in an argument, you can then examine it. For example, consider the argument, "We should have capital punishment because criminals will commit fewer crimes if they think they might be executed."

EVALUATING VALUE
STATEMENTS

---

1. *Separate the argument into its factual and value parts.*
   Factual part:
   Capital punishment will make criminals commit fewer crimes. (Notice that this could be investigated by examining statistics on the number of crimes with and without capital punishment.)
   Value assumption:
   Fewer crimes is good (a desirable outcome).
2. *Rephrase the value statement into general terms.*
   Anything (general term) which causes fewer crimes is good (value judgment).
3. *Ask yourself if the value statement is right in all instances.*
   Is the statement, "Anything which causes fewer crimes is good" true? Can you think of cases in which you might not agree? Substitute some specific situations and see if the statement is still right. For example, "Jailing all people accused of a crime, whether found guilty or not, would also cause fewer crimes to be committed. Should we do this?"

This kind of questioning will help both you and the person who originally made the claim think more fully about the value(s) behind the claim.

Three general questions can be used to test the worthiness of value claims.
- Are you willing to use this value in all situations?
- What would society be like if everyone believed and acted on this value?
- Would you want the value applied to you?

The next page contains two charts you may find helpful for reminding you of methods you can use to analyze the viewpoints presented in this book. As you proceed, refer to this "Guide to Critical Thinking" to help you with the lessons.

A MODEL FOR ANALYZING ARGUMENTS

A model is a way of organizing information. One type of model is an acronym where each letter in the model stands for a word. The model outlined here is **ARMEAR**. Each letter will remind you of a part of arguments to examine.

A   Author
- Who wrote this interpretation and why?
- What are the author's values or beliefs?
- What can you learn about the author?

R   Relevant Information
- What do you know about the topic being argued or topics related to it?

M   Main Point
- What is the main point or thesis of the argument?

E   Evidence
- What evidence is presented to support the argument?
- How reliable is it?
- What are the sources of the evidence?

A   Assumptions
- What assumptions does the author make?

R   Reasoning
- What reasoning is used in the argument? Cause and effect? Comparison? Generalization? Proof? Debate?
- How strong is the reasoning?

FIVE MAIN PARTS OF AN ARGUMENT

Assertion, main point, or thesis
- What is the author trying to prove?

Evidence
- Is the source given for information?
- How strong is it? Primary? Reason to distort? Other evidence to verify? Public or private? (**PROP**).

Reasoning
- Cause and Effect — Is the connection shown? Are there other possible causes? Is there an important cause previous to the one proposed?
- Comparisons — How are the two cases different and how are they similar?
- Generalizations — How large and representative is the sample?
- Proof — Does the evidence support the point being made? How many examples are given? Is this authority an expert on this topic?
- Debate — Does the author attack other views in a fair way? Have all possible alternatives been eliminated?

Assumptions
- What must be true if the thesis is true (acceptable)?

Values
- Do I agree with these values?
- Is this value position right in all instances?

LESSON 1   Identifying Sources

When someone makes a claim or states an opinion, you should require that person to give information (often examples), as well as to provide the source of the information. The source is the person, written document, or object from which the information came. The source may also be the person making the claim, based on his or her own observations or experiences.

> When evaluating claims or opinions, you should ask the person:
> * What information do you have to support your claims?
> * From what source did you get the information?

Q Label each item below with the appropriate letter.

S   A **source** of information is given.

N   **No** source of information is given.

_____ 1.   Students aren't working as hard as they used to. They are lazy.

_____ 2.   Students are lazier than they used to be. This is shown in their test scores, which have declined steadily in the past five years.

_____ 3.   The Spanish mistreated the Aztec Indians, making slaves of many of them.

_____ 4.   The printing press had an important effect on European society. According to a recent book by Neil Postman, the printing press allowed thousands of Europeans to begin reading about new areas and new ideas.

_____ 5.   The Spanish treated the Indians cruelly. Hernando Cortez, the leader of the Spanish conquest of Mexico City, even admits this in his reports.

_____ 6.   The French colonies in America were sparsely settled. For example, in the 1750s the English had twenty times as many colonists as the French.

_____ 7.   English sea dogs made a great deal of money by raiding Spanish ships. For example, Sir Francis Drake returned from his 1572–1573 raids on Spanish ships with £40,000 (about $1,200,000 today) in stolen treasure.[1]

_____ 8.   Richard Hakluyt pushed England to give government support for colonizing America. In *Discourse on Western Planting,* Hakluyt stressed the military advantages of "the plantinge of two or three strong fortes" along the Atlantic Coast of North America.

---

[1] A.L. Rowse, *The Elizabethans and America* (New York, 1959), pp. 179–80.

LESSON 2   Evaluating Sources

Primary Sources

A *primary source* is evidence (often written) given by a person who was part of or present at the event reported. A primary source may also be an object that was a part of the event.

To determine the type of source, ask yourself:
- Were the people doing the reporting part of the event?
- Did they see the event they are reporting on?

If so, it is a primary source.

Q Label each item below with the appropriate letter.

     P   The source is a **primary** source.

     S   The source is a **secondary** source.

_____ 1.   Terry said she saw Dasha buy the sneakers.

_____ 2.   This book, *The United States* by Winthrop Jordan and other historians, published in 1982, states that Giovanni da Verrazano explored the Atlantic Coast of North America for the French in 1524.

_____ 3.   Roger Williams wrote that he had to work very hard when he went to Rhode Island.

_____ 4.   In 1616 Samuel deChamplain described the Canadian Indians he met this way: "Their life is a miserable one in comparison to our own, but they are happy."

_____ 5.   A newspaper in England stated that farmland in the American colonies was very fertile.

_____ 6.   Reggie said that he read in his history textbook that children in colonial America worked hard.

_____ 7.   James Oglethorpe said that the land where he settled in colonial Georgia was beautiful.

_____ 8.   The 1756 indenture papers (the contract that made him an indentured servant) of Isaiah Thomas show that he worked for a printer.

[Continued on next page.]

[Continued from previous page.]
Reason to Lie

People have a *reason to lie* when their statements make themselves or their group look good or when they help their own interests (for example, when they make more money). People generally have no reason to lie when they (usually without realizing it) make themselves look bad or their enemy look good.

> When questioning the truthfulness of an argument, ask yourself:
> - Does the statement make the speaker (or the group) look good?
> - Does the statement further or improve the interests of the speaker (or the group)?

Q Label each item below with the appropriate letter.

R   The person has a **reason to lie**.

N   The person has **no** reason to lie.

_____ 9.   Bill said he didn't steal the radio.

_____ 10. The Pilgrims said they would not have survived without the help of friendly Indians, such as Squanto. (Assume that most colonists did not like Indians.)

_____ 11. Captain John Smith said in 1614 that he generally caught 200–300 cod in one day.

_____ 12. William Penn said that his colony, Pennsylvania, was the best colony in North America.

_____ 13. The police found the stolen radio in Emilie's locker. (The evidence is the radio).

Corroboration

Corroboration means finding other evidence that supports evidence you already have. For example, if I claim that Gabriel was a great baseball player, and you find a newspaper article saying that Gabriel was a great baseball player, you have corroborated what I said.

Q What evidence might you search for to corroborate or verify the evidence in:

14.   statement 5 (page 20)?

15.   statement 12 (above)?

LESSON 3   Determining Causes and Effects

> • An *effect* is an event or situation which results from something.
> • A *cause* is a reason for a result or a thing which brings about an effect.

Q Label the items in each group below with the appropriate letter. (The first one is done for you as an example.)

    C   This portion of the statement is the **cause**.
    E   This portion of the statement is the **effect**.

_E_ 1.   The game was cancelled

_C_ 2.   due to bad weather.

_____ 3.   The track coach told Almaz she could be a good runner,

_____ 4.   so she decided to try out for the team.

_____ 5.   Colonists in America had more freedom than people in Europe

_____ 6.   because there was so much land in America.

_____ 7.   The poor location of the Jamestown colony

_____ 8.   led to the "starving time" which almost wiped the colony out.

Q For each of the following situations, think of as many possible causes as you can, then evaluate the strength of the argument given.

9.   Why do students get bad grades? List all the reasons you can think of.

"William gets bad grades because none of the teachers like him."

    a.   How strong do you think the above explanation is?

    b.   Support your opinion.

[Continued on next page.]

[Continued from previous page.]

10. Why are some people good athletes? List all the reasons you can think of.

"Use the new 'He-Man Universal Gym' and become a good athlete."

    a. How strong do you think the above explanation is?

    b. Support your opinion.

11. Why do some individuals, groups, or countries explore other parts of the world? List all the reasons you can think of.

"There were a number of factors which led Europeans to explore other parts of the world in the 1400s and 1500s. First, strong national states had arisen in Europe, and national states had the money to finance such risky adventures. Second, Europeans wanted new trade routes to China to get the goods they desired. Third, many countries were greedy to get more gold and silver, so they sent out expeditions in search of the two metals."

    a. How strong do you think the above explanation is?

    b. Support your opinion.

LESSON 4   Evaluating Cause-and-Effect Relationships

Suppose Mr. Perez argues that all cities that have fire departments also have fires, so the fire departments must be the reason for the fires. This causal argument is weak because Mr. Perez does not explain how (or why) fire departments would cause fires—and it is very difficult to think of a good reason why they would.

When considering causal arguments, you should ask:
- Do the people making them show how the cause(s) led to the effect?
- If not, is it reasonable to believe that the cause(s) led to the effect?

Q Label each item below with the appropriate letter, then explain your answer in the space provided.

S   There is a **strong** connection between the cause and effect.

R   There may be a **reasonable** connection between the cause and effect, but it is not explained well in this argument.

W   There is a **weak** connection between the cause and effect.

_____ 1.   Larry: "I know my car stopped because it ran out of gas. The fuel gauge reads empty."

_____ 2.   Smoking causes lung cancer.

_____ 3.   Jennie: "Whenever I study for science tests I do poorly on them, but when I don't study I do well. I'm going to stop studying so I will do well on all of them."

_____ 4.   Tests show that the tar and nicotine in cigarette smoke causes irritation of lung tissue which leads to cancer. Thus, smoking causes lung cancer.

[Continued on next page.]

[Continued from previous page.]

_____ 5.   Diseases brought by the Spanish reduced the Indian population of Mexico by 90% during the last half of the sixteenth century.

_____ 6.   Colonists in Virginia grew and exported so much tobacco in the 1600s because tobacco was easy to plant and cultivate.

_____ 7.   The French got along well with the Indians because they intermarried with them.

_____ 8.   In the 1500s the Indian population of the Western Hemisphere had had no contact with the diseases of Europe. When Spaniards came to Mexico, the Indians there had no immunities (defenses of the body) against such diseases as smallpox and measles. As a result, 90% of the Indians died within fifty years.

_____ 9.   Indians in New England were angered by the English colonists taking their land. This anger led to King Philip's War, in which the Indians attacked fifty-two Puritan villages.

LESSON 5   Recognizing and Assessing Cause-and-Effect Reasoning

Q To be cause-and-effect reasoning, the statement has to argue that something caused, led to, or brought about something else. Label each item below with the appropriate letter.

> **C**   Item illustrates **cause-and-effect reasoning**.
> **N**   Item does **not** illustrate cause-and-effect reasoning.

If cause-and-effect reasoning is shown in the argument, identify the cause and the effect in the space provided beneath each item.

_____ 1.   By increasing the number of books and reducing their cost, the printing press stimulated the desire to read, helped spread the new ideas of the Renaissance, and aroused interest in distant lands. In this way, the printing press was an important factor leading to exploration.

CAUSE: EFFECT:

_____ 2.   The League of the Iroquois in upstate New York was a political alliance of Indians which lasted for a remarkably long time. It made decisions about war and diplomacy.

CAUSE: EFFECT:

_____ 3.   Eastern Woodland Indians used lightweight birch-bark canoes.

CAUSE: EFFECT:

_____ 4.   The Spanish population in California was very small in 1804. This was due in part to the Spanish government's failure to encourage their citizens to settle in California.

CAUSE: EFFECT:

_____ 5.   Columbus landed in San Salvador and then explored other Caribbean Islands, including Cuba. Despite great evidence to the contrary, Columbus continued to think he was in Asia, near China.

CAUSE: EFFECT:

_____ 6.   The French got along with Indians better than the English did.

CAUSE: EFFECT:

[Continued on next page.]

[Continued from previous page.]

 Fill in the diagram for each cause-and-effect argument below, then use the information in the diagram to evaluate the strength of the argument.

7.   Maxine notices that when ice cream sales are high, crime rates are also high (which is true). She concludes that something in the ice cream causes criminal behavior.

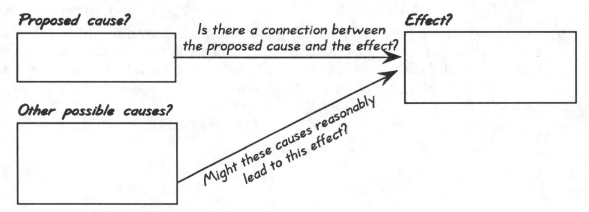

How strong is Maxine's reasoning? Why do you think so?

8.   The Spanish Empire declined primarily because of the defeat of the Spanish Armada. Once the Spanish could no longer control the ocean, they couldn't bring back to Spain the enormous wealth of the New World. Without the wealth Spain got weaker.

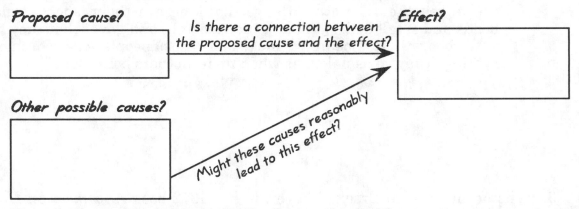

How strong is this reasoning? Why do you think so?

LESSON 6   Evaluating Evidence About the Colonies

 Evaluate the following pieces of evidence by listing strengths and weaknesses of each. If you need help, refer to the section on **Evidence** in the "Guide to Critical Thinking" (Unit 1), especially the **PROP** method.

1. In *Generall Historie of Virginia*, published in England in 1624, John Smith wrote that, before he took over as their leader, colonists at Jamestown argued too much and didn't work hard. He said that he saved the colony by taking over in 1608 and providing strong leadership. He stopped a lot of the arguing and made everyone work hard.

    STRENGTHS: WEAKNESSES:

2. On October 12, 1492, Christopher Columbus, in his *Journal of the First Voyage of Columbus*, wrote about his first contacts with the "natives" (Indians) of San Salvadore:

    "[Since] I knew that they were a people who could be more easily freed and converted to our holy faith by love than by force, [I] gave to some of them red caps and glass beads to put round their necks, and many other things of little value, which gave them great pleasure and made them so much our friends that it was a marvel to see. They afterwards came to the ship's boats where we were, swimming and bringing us parrots, cotton threads in skeins, darts, and many other things; and we exchanged them for other things that we gave them, such as glass beads and small bells. [At last], they took all, and gave what they had with good will. It appeared to me to be a race of people very poor in everything. They go as naked as when their mothers bore them."

    STRENGTHS: WEAKNESSES:

3. Historian Rebecca Brooks Gruver, in her 1972 book *An American History*, describes William Penn as a good leader. Historians Lewis Todd and Merle Curti also describe Penn as a good leader.

    STRENGTHS: WEAKNESSES:

LESSON 7   What Happened to Roanoke?

 This problem is about the lost colony of Roanoke. Your job is to figure out, like a historical detective, what might have happened to the lost colony. Begin by listing reasons that a colony in America in the 1500s might fail and disappear.

Background Information

More than twenty years before the first Englishmen landed in Jamestown—and more than thirty years before the Pilgrims settled in Plymouth—groups of colonists tried three times to found a permanent English colony at Roanoke Island, off the coast of present-day North Carolina (see the map on page 31).

In 1585 the first colony on Roanoke was established by 108 men, but many died and the rest were taken back to England by Sir Francis Drake in 1586.

The month after these colonists had left, a relief ship filled with supplies for Roanoke arrived at the island. The ship returned to England, but left seventeen men on the island to protect England's claim to North America.

In July of 1587 John White led 117 colonists in the third attempt to establish a permanent colony. When these colonists landed at Roanoke, they found no trace of the seventeen men who had been left there the previous year.

These colonists soon realized that they would need more supplies, and it was too late in the year to plant crops. They voted to send their governor, John White, to England to get supplies. White sailed to England but could not return to the colony because England was in a naval war with Spain at the time. (The Spanish Armada fought the British in 1588.) He did not return to Roanoke until August 1590—three years after he had left. White found no colonists on the island, although he did find the remains of houses, broken pieces of armor, iron bars, and some heavier things, along with some grasses and rotten trees burning in a fire pit.

Before the governor left Roanoke in 1587, he and the colonists had agreed on a way to leave messages. If the colonists had to leave the island, they would carve on a tree the name of the place they had gone. If there was danger, they would carve a cross above the name. In 1590 White found CROATOAN carved on one tree and CRO on another. No cross was carved on either tree. Croatoan was the name of a nearby island (see map) and also of a group of Indians.

Unfortunately, the anchors on Governor White's ship had been lost during a storm, and he could not stop at Croatoan Island before returning to England. He was never to return to Croatoan or Roanoke to find his family or the rest of the colonists.

[Continued on next page.]

[Continued from previous page.]

Relevant Information About Roanoke

1. Croatoan Indians were friendly with the Roanoke colonists when John White was there in 1587.

2. William Strachey, secretary of the Jamestown colony, wrote in *Historie of Travell into Virginia Britania* (around 1608–1609) that the King of England knew "that the men, women and children of the first plantation [colony] at Roanoke were by practice and commandment of Powhatan [chief of the Powhatan Indians of the Chesapeake Bay area, about 80 miles north of Roanoke] miserably slaughtered without any offence given him."

3. The Spanish have no record of attacking Roanoke Island before 1590. Spanish soldiers did land at Roanoke Island sometime in late 1590, after John White had returned to England for the second time, and found no colonists there.

4. In 1605 a group of English ships was captured by the Spanish off the coast of South Carolina. Instructions for the voyage, written in England in 1604, directed the ships to stop at Croatoan Island, where Englishmen were supposedly settled.

5. Samuel Purchas wrote in 1625 in *Hakluytus Posthumus*, "Powhatan confessed that he had been at the murder of that colony and showed to Captain Smith a musket barrel and a bronze mortar and certain pieces of iron which had been theirs."

6. In 1603 Sir Walter Raleigh employed men in two ships to sail to the Chesapeake Bay to look for the Lost Colony of Roanoke.

7. In 1719 white hunters said they found Indians called the Croatoan tribe in Robeson County, North Carolina, about 200 miles from Roanoke Island. These Indians were light skinned, had blue eyes, spoke the type of English that had been spoken in England in the late 1500s, and had some of the same family names as those of the Roanoke colonists.

8. The area around Roanoke Island is very dangerous for sailing. It is known as "the graveyard of the Atlantic."

9. When exploring the area in 1585, some Roanoke colonists met Chesapeake Indians. These colonists reported that they stayed at the Skicoac Village and that the Indians were friendly with them.

10. The Roanoke colonists discussed with John White the possibility of moving inland while he was gone. They said they would divide, leaving a person (or a group, it is unclear which) on Roanoke Island to meet him upon his return.

11. The Roanoke colonists had one regular-sized ship, called a *pinnace*, with them. A ship of this type could not have held all the colonists with their supplies and equipment.

[Continued on next page.]

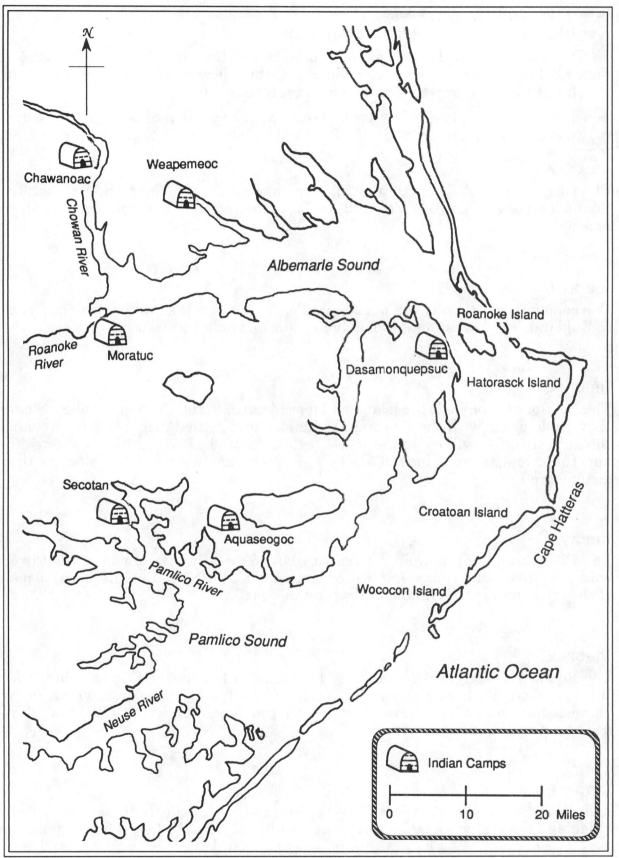

Figure 1, Map of Roanoke Region in the 1500s

[Continued on next page.]

[Continued from previous page.]

Evaluating Theories About Roanoke

There are several theories of what happened to the Lost Colony of Roanoke. A *theory*, which is like a hypothesis or interpretation, is an explanation of something which has not been proven true beyond a reasonable doubt.

 In the space provided, write and explain your opinion of that theory. Whenever possible, refer to specific Relevant Information to support your opinion.

Theory A

The whole colony at Roanoke was killed in an attack by the Spanish. After all, the Spanish were at war with England at the time, and they had soldiers and ships nearby in Florida.

Theory B

The colonists at Roanoke ran out of supplies, so they built small boats to sail back to England. The boats sank, probably in a storm, and no one survived.

Theory C

The Roanoke Colony left the island and moved north to the Chesapeake Bay. There they made peace with the Chesapeake Indians and settled near Skicoac, probably the largest Indian village in the whole region. Around 1607 both the Chesapeakes and the colonists were massacred by the Powhatan Indians. The colonists thus disappeared.

Theory D

The Roanoke Colony moved to Croatoan Island (see the map), where they lived with the Croatoan Indians. Later they intermarried with the Indians, became part of the tribe, and moved inland when the Indians did.

Theory E

The Roanoke Colony was taken away by aliens, either from UFOs or from under the sea. Roanoke Island is within the Bermuda Triangle, an area where many planes, ships, and people have mysteriously vanished. The letters CRO may have been a reference to the aliens.

Theory F

The colonists on Roanoke Island were attacked by hostile Indians. Some were killed and the rest were taken away as servants, never to be heard from again.

© 1990 MIDWEST PUBLICATIONS, P.O. Box 448, Pacific Grove, CA 93950

LESSON 8   Did Pocahontas Really Rescue Captain John Smith?

Background Information

Captain John Smith, one of the earliest heroes in American history, came to Jamestown with the first settlers. His strong leadership may have been the major reason this first settlement survived the difficulties of the first year.

John Smith was quite an adventurer. One of his most well-known exploits happened in 1607, when Pocahontas rescued him from being killed by her father, the Indian chief Powhatan. There is some question, however, whether this dramatic rescue ever took place. Some historians believe Smith made up the story.

Historians do not always agree about what happened in the past. They write theories or hypotheses of what happened. In history these hypotheses are called "interpretations."

Two interpretations of the Pocahontas-John Smith episode are presented in this lesson. Since each is believed by several historians, they are called, respectively, Interpretation A and Interpretation B. Read each interpretation and its evidence then decide whether Pocahontas did, in fact, rescue Captain John Smith from death.

Relevant Information

1. In *A True Discourse of the Present State of Virginia*, published in 1615, author Raphe Hamor did not mention the Pocahontas incident at all. Hamor was one of the leaders in Jamestown, knew Pocahontas well, and referred to her several times in his book.

2. Other people in Jamestown said that Smith and two others were attacked by Indians. The two others were killed, and Smith was held by Powhatan for several days. On Smith's return to Jamestown, he was arrested for having permitted the death of his two companions.

3. The following story about the famous explorer De Soto was published in 1609. De Soto was supposedly captured by the Indians and brought before their chief, Utica.

    "By command of [Indian Chief] Utica, De Soto was bound hand and foot to four stakes...that he might be burned; but a daughter of the chief pleaded that he might be spared. Though one Christian, she said, might do no good, certainly he could do no harm, and it would be an honor to have one for a captive; to which the father agreed, directing the injuries of De Soto to be healed."

[Continued on next page.]

[Continued from previous page.]

Captain John Smith: Interpretation A

(1) The rescue of Captain John Smith by Pocahontas in 1607 is one of the great tales in American history. In truth, however, John Smith was not saved by Pocahontas. The Indians actually were friendly with him and let him go after four days. In his book *True Relation*, Smith said that Powhatan assured him of the Indians' friendship and gave him food to eat.[1]

(2) It wasn't until 1624, when Smith wrote his *Generall Historie of Virginia*, that the first mention of the Pocahontas rescue appeared.[2] Obviously, he made the story up to make himself look good. After all, before her death in the 1620s, Pocahontas had become famous in London, and Smith could gain some of that popularity by saying that the beautiful Indian had rescued him.

(3) Also, since Smith was a constant liar, his word can't be trusted. For example, although he claimed to have been involved in European wars in Hungary and Transylvania against the Turks, many of the names he mentioned in those tales didn't exist. There is no evidence to show that the main characters in Smith's story—an English Jesuit, Lord Ebersbaught, Baron Kissell, or Henry Volda—ever existed. Smith also claimed that in one battle he single-handedly killed and beheaded three Turkish soldiers.[3] This is ridiculous!

(4) Smith also wrote often of the many women who fell in love with him, and on at least two other occasions, he claimed that beautiful women had rescued him.[4]

(5) The biggest flaw in the Pocahontas tale is that if such a daring rescue had taken place, why did Smith fail to mention it in his book *True Relation*, which was printed only the next year? Did he forget about it? Why, then, did he remember it seventeen years later when he wrote his *Generall Historie of Virginia*?

(6) The answer is that the rescue by Pocahontas never took place. It was a story made up by a liar who wanted to raise his reputation as an adventurer and a ladies' man.

Endnotes for Interpretation A

[1] John Smith, *True Relation*, 1608 (Rewritten in modern English) "Arriving at Weramocomoco, their Emperor (Powhatan) was proudly lying upon a bedstead a foot high.... He kindly welcomed me with good words and great platters of food, assuring me of his friendship, and of letting me go within four days."

[2] John Smith, *Generall Historie of Virginia*, 1624, Reprinted in Henry Johnson, *Teaching of History* (New York: Macmillan, 1940), p. 309.
"At last the Indians brought me to Meronocomo, where Powhatan their Emperor was. Before a fire upon a seat like a bedstead, he sat covered with a great robe.... Having given me the best food that such barbarous people could offer, a long discussion was held, but the conclusion was, two great stones were brought before Powhatan: then as many Indians as could laid hands on me and dragged their clubs to beat out my brains. Pocahontas, the King's dearest daughter, when no plea for mercy could stop the murder, got my head in her arms, and laid her...head upon mine to save me from death: Whereas the Emperor [Powhatan] was contented that I should live to make him hatchets, and her bells, beads, and copper."

[3] Lewis L. Kropf, a Hungarian historian, compared Captain Smith's accounts of his adventures in Europe in the Turkish wars against Hungarian documents about the wars with the Turks. Kropf concluded that the places and people mentioned in Smith's writing were pure fictions.

[4] John Smith wrote that he escaped in a small boat from a band of pirates and was rescued by the beautiful Lady Chanoyes. At another time, Smith wrote that some barbarians attacked him. He managed to escape and was nursed back to health by the beautiful Lady Callamata.

[Continued on next page.]

[Continued from previous page.]

Captain John Smith: Interpretation B

(1) Captain John Smith's rescue by Pocahontas in 1607 is one of the great stories in early American history. Recently, however, some historians have questioned whether the event actually took place. These historians argue that Smith was a notorious liar who made up the rescue story to make himself look better. But these historians are wrong. Recent evidence shows that Smith was not a liar and that the Pocahontas rescue probably happened the way the Captain reported it.

(2) First, while Smith did not mention the rescue in his book *True Relation*, printed in 1608, there are several explanations for this. The publisher, who, after all, said that there were other parts which he decided not to include,[1] may have left it out of the manuscript. Also, in 1608 Smith may not have thought the rescue important enough to mention. Thus, there may be good reason why Smith failed to mention the incident in the book.

(3) Second, some of Smith's more questioned stories turn out to be very accurate. In his accounts of wars in Hungary and Transylvania (parts of Europe) against the Turks, he refers to people who historians believe didn't exist. In fact, they did exist. There was an English Jesuit involved named William Wright; "Lord Ebersbaught" was Carl Von Herbertsdorf; "Baron Kissel" was Hanns Khisl; Volda was the noble, Folta. Smith wrote in 1602 that "Volda" completed his twentieth year in military service, which is exactly right. Other historians thought the people Smith mentioned didn't exist because Smith misspelled so many of their names [2]

(4) Smith's story which stated that he cut off the heads of three Turkish soldiers has also been proven true. Szamoskoezy, a person from that time, reported that Smith killed the three Turks in duels during a siege on a city—exactly the way the Captain described the events.

(5) Smith's accuracy in writing about the wars against the Turks, as well as other reports, shows him to be not only a brave and capable fighter, but also a truthful and reliable reporter of events. Although we have only Smith's account of the Pocahontas rescue story, we can depend on his accuracy as to what happened.

Endnotes for Interpretation B

[1] John Smith, *True Relation*, 1608. [For the full quotation, see endnote 1 of Interpretation A.] In the introduction of *True Relation*, the publisher wrote, "Somewhat more was written by Smith, which being as I thought [fit only to be private] I would not venture to make it public [publish it]."

[2] Laura Polanyi Striker, a historian trained in Hungary, found all the names mentioned by Smith in her study of Hungarian documents. She also found the information about Folta completing his twentieth year of service in 1602.

 Did Pocahontas really rescue John Smith? Explain your answer.

[Continued on next page.]

[Continued from previous page.]
Worksheet: Interpretations on John Smith
Q **Interpretation A**

_____ 1. Which of the following best describes the main point of Interpretation A?
- A. John Smith was not involved in the Turkish wars.
- B. John Smith wanted to be famous.
- C. The *Generall Historie of Virginia* is inaccurate.
- D. The Pocahontas rescue never took place.

2. List two pieces of evidence given in this interpretation. (Remember, evidence is statements by witnesses, written documents, or objects. Evidence is information which gives a source.)
- A.

- B.

3. Why is Smith's truthfulness about his adventures in the Turkish wars important to determining whether Pocahontas really rescued him?

4. Paragraph 4 calls attention to other times that Smith had claimed he was rescued by beautiful women. Is this point important to this interpretation? If so, why?

Q **Interpretation B**

5. What is the main point of Interpretation B?

6. List two pieces of evidence presented in this argument:
- A.

- B.

7. Why is the report by Szamoskoezy (paragraph 4) important?

[Continued on next page.]

 © 1990 MIDWEST PUBLICATIONS, P.O. Box 448, Pacific Grove, CA 93950

[Continued from previous page.]

 General Questions

8. Compare Captain Smith's two accounts of his capture (endnotes 1 and 2 for Interpretation A). Look at the factual details. Other than the rescue difference, are the details the same? If they are the same, what does this tell you about Smith? If not, what does it show?

9. Look at the **Relevant Information** (RI) on page 27. How does each piece of information affect your view of whether or not the Pocahontas rescue incident actually occurred?

    RI 1

    RI 2

    RI 3

10. How could you check further on this topic to help you decide whether the rescue actually took place? For what information would you look? What questions would you try to answer?

LESSON 9   How Did Immigration to Colonial Maryland Affect the Lives of Women?

Background Information

A move across the ocean to a new environment would have brought important changes for both men and women in the 1600s. Keep in mind that America was, at that time, still a vast wilderness. Life in England, although still based mostly on farming, was much more settled than life in America.

This lesson is about how the move from England to Maryland in the 1600s may have changed the way women lived. Read the **Relevant Information** below, then answer the questions on the following pages about how emigration to colonial America may have affected the lives of the women.

Relevant Information

The following factors were important to women's lives in England in the 1600s.

1. In the eyes of the law, the husband owned all the property, including any properties the wife brought into the marriage.

2. The average age of men and women at marriage was 25.

3. People lived near their relatives. To a significant degree, these relatives controlled the social conduct of young people, for example, courtship (dating).

4. On average, women lived somewhat longer than men.

5. When men died, they usually left their property to adult sons. In the majority of cases, they left it to the sons with instructions to support their mother.

The following factors were important to the lives of women who came to Maryland in the 1600s.

6. Almost everyone was an immigrant to America. Very few people were born in Maryland.

7. There were three men for every woman in Maryland.

8. A great majority (85%) of the immigrants were indentured servants. Indentured servants worked for someone else for five to seven years to pay back a debt.

9. Women were, on average, 25 years old when they married. Men were several years older when they married.

10. Men would expect to live to age 43; women died younger.

11. Married women generally outlived their husbands because they were younger than their husbands.

12. One marriage partner was likely to die within seven years of the marriage.

13. Only half of the children born in Maryland would live to adulthood (age 20).

[Continued on next page.]

[Continued from previous page.]
Projecting Effects

 One part of causal reasoning is projecting effects. When you project effects, you must be careful to explain how the given circumstances (causes) would have led to each effect you suggest. Think of as many effects as you can. Sometimes those you don't think of at first will be more important, cancelling out the earlier effects you thought of.

1. Write as many effects as you can think of that might have happened to women because they emigrated to Maryland in the 1600s, then project effects for each of those effects.

Effects	**Effects of those effects**
a.	a.
b.	b.
c.	c.

2. Native-born daughters of women who immigrated to Maryland in the 1600s married much younger than their mothers had, possibly averaging around sixteen years of age at their marriage. List several effects of these earlier marriages, project effects of those effects, then try projecting further effects.

Effects	**Effects of effects**	**Further effects**
a.	a.	a.
b.	b.	b.
c.	c.	c.

 Based on what you learned in this lesson, mark each of the following statements "T" if you feel reasonably confident it is a true statement. Leave the others blank. Remember to base your answer on information you learned in this lesson.

_____ 3.   In the 1600s colonial American women had more economic and social independence than European women.

_____ 4.   There was a low life expectancy in the world in the 1600s.

_____ 5.   Marriages didn't last long in Maryland.

_____ 6.   Women generally outlived their husbands throughout the Chesapeake Region (Virginia and Maryland).

_____ 7.   Most Maryland widows remarried quickly.

[Continued on next page.]

[Continued from previous page.]
Making Generalizations: Little Circles and Big Circles

When you know something about a certain group (in this case women in Maryland in the 1600s), you have to be careful about how far you generalize your knowledge. Look at the diagram in Figure 2, below.

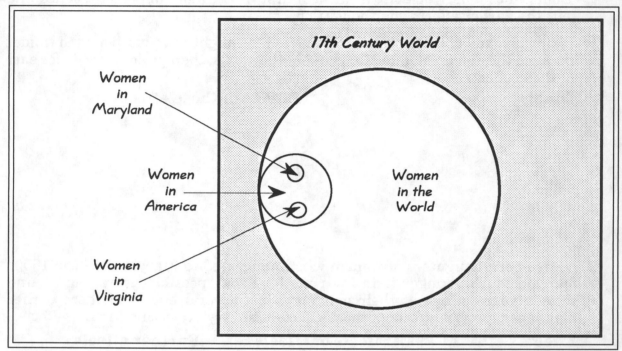

Figure 2: The 17th Century World

The information in this lesson concerned only one of the innermost circles of Figure 2. What was true for Maryland women in the 1600s may or may not have also been true for Virginia women in the 1600s. It would only be true if all the significant conditions were the same or similar. If most women who immigrated to Virginia were not indentured servants or if they married younger, then you cannot say with any confidence that what you know about colonial women in Maryland applies to colonial women in Virginia.

> The important question to ask yourself is: "Does the part or sample that I know about represent the whole group well?"

Now, look back at your answers on the previous page. In light of this information on generalizations, change any you wish. Be ready to explain why you changed your mind.

LESSON 10   What Caused the Salem Witch Hysteria?

Background Information

In the cold winter months of 1691–1692, several teenage girls gathered at the home of Reverend Samuel Parris, the minister and religious leader of Salem Village. Here, they listened to tales of the supernatural from Reverend Parris's slave, Tituba.

In January 1692 some of these girls began to behave oddly. A doctor was called in who (since he was unable to explain the strange behavior) suggested that witchcraft might be the cause. A number of other girls soon joined the original group and began accusing people from the surrounding area of bewitching them. In the public hearings (called examinations) the girls screamed and went through contortions as they pointed out their tormentors. A sense of hysteria gripped the whole colony.

Salem Village (in the present location of Danvers, Massachusetts) was, in some respects, part of Salem Town (today's Salem, Massachusetts) in 1692. Villagers paid taxes to the town, and many villagers traded with and through the town. In other respects, however, Salem Village was independent from Salem Town. By 1692 the village had its own minister and meeting house, which made it a separate congregation—and a separate community from Salem Town.

In June of 1692, the governor of Massachusetts established a special court to try the witchcraft cases in Salem Town. The judges of this court were political leaders appointed by the governor. None of the judges was a minister, although one had been.

Before the hysteria died down in the autumn of 1692, nineteen persons had been hanged and one man had been pressed to death. Eight more were under sentence of death, 50 awaited sentencing, and 150 were in jail awaiting trial when they were pardoned.

Almost everyone in the 1600s believed in witchcraft. During the years 1300–1600, probably a half million people were killed as alleged witches in England alone.

The common belief of the time was that someone became a witch by signing the "Devil's Book." He or she would then go to black masses where, among other things, Christian prayers were said backwards. (This is why a witch was not supposed to be able to say the Lord's Prayer without making a mistake.)

Witches also were presumed to have a "familiar," such as a cat or dog, which served as a messenger from the devil. On the witch's body was something called a "Devil's Mark" (a spot where the devil or a familiar sucked the blood of the witch, thereby feeding on the witch's soul). Accused witches were examined for such a mark.

Once someone became a witch (males were called witches or wizards; "warlock" was rarely used), his or her spirit (also called an "apparition" or "specter") could move out of the witch's physical body and torment other people. The court of 1692 accepted the testimony of witnesses that the specters of accused witches had tormented them. Such testimony was called "spectral evidence."

Many people who practiced witchcraft at this time used puppets to hurt people they didn't like. The witch would stick pins into the doll and the targeted person would feel pain or have other physical symptoms. Although this was similar to voodoo as practiced in Haiti, it was different from voodoo in that it was not intended to be as serious.

[Continued on next page.]

Salem Witch Hysteria: Relevant Information

[Note: English usage in all quotations has been modernized.]

1. Salem Village was about five miles northwest of Salem Town. In 1692 it had 90 houses and about 550 people. (See Figure 3, p. 47.)

2. In addition to farming, some people took up such "winter" occupations as weavers, brickmakers, coopers (barrel makers), and sellers of alcoholic beverages (tavern owners).

3. The people in Salem Village were mostly farmers and had a reputation for quarreling and being stubborn. Their disputes often involved land or church controversies and resulted in ill feelings and long-lasting resentments.

4. Local church disputes were famous in colonial history. From as early as 1672, two groups in Salem Village had carried on controversies over the Village minister. One minister, George Burroughs, was denied his salary.

5. Samuel Parris took over as minister of Salem Village in 1689.

6. Increase Mather, one of the most influential ministers in Massachusetts, challenged the evidence accepted in the Salem Trials. In a sermon to other ministers in Cambridge on October 3, 1692, he criticized the Court's acceptance of spectral evidence, claiming, "Better that ten suspected witches should escape than that one innocent person should be condemned."

7. There is no evidence regarding what the accused believed would happen to them if they confessed. In some previous cases, the courts delayed execution when the accused confessed; most were, nevertheless, executed. People in Salem may have believed they could escape execution by confessing.

8. Petty neighbor disputes had helped cause several earlier witchcraft episodes.

9. Although the Salem witchcraft episode was much larger than any other episode in the colonies (because of the large numbers participating and the large numbers hanged), it was small compared to European witch hysterias.

10. In most Salem Witchcraft Trial cases, the accuser and the accused person did not live next to each other and did not know each other well.

11. Reverend Samuel Willard is believed to have anonymously published a pamphlet in 1692 in which he condemned the use of spectral evidence and denounced the accusers as "liars."

12. On June 15, 1692, a group of Boston ministers led by Cotton Mather sent a letter to Governor Phips and his council. The letter urged vigorous prosecution of proven witches but recommended "a very critical and exquisite caution" in the use of spectral evidence.

13. Some of the people who were accused of witchcraft and some of those who were hanged as witches were outcasts in Salem Village. Others, such as Rebecca Nurse, were respected members of the community and of the church.

14. Some people who were accused of witchcraft and some people who were hanged for it lived in Salem Village, but most of the accused did not.

15. One of the afflicted girls, Betty Parris, took no part in the examinations or trials because her father, Reverend Parris, sent her away. Her younger brother, who was born in 1692, later died insane.

16. One of the afflicted girls accused John Proctor's wife of being a witch. Adults who heard the accusation were skeptical of it, and the girl responded, "It [the accusation] was for sport. I must have some sport."

[Continued on next page.]

[Continued from previous page.]

17. In 1720 three sisters in Littletown, Massachusetts, claimed that a witch in town was causing them headaches. There was no trial, and in 1728 the oldest sister admitted that the girls had made up the story to get attention. She said they had picked the woman they accused at random.

18. During the trial of Sarah Good, one of the afflicted girls presented part of a broken knife blade with which she said Sarah had tormented her. A boy then came forward, said the blade part was from his knife, and showed that the broken piece of blade fit perfectly. The judge told the afflicted girl to stick to the facts and had her continue her testimony.

19. Reverend Parris took the official notes at witchcraft examinations and trials.

20. In 1706 Ann Putnam, Jr. admitted that she had been used as an instrument of the devil in the Salem Witch Trials.

21. Robert Calef criticized Cotton and Increase Mather on many occasions other than the witchcraft trials.

22. When accused witches were released from jail in late 1692, the afflicted girls did not become tormented again.

23. In his book *Major Symptoms of Hysteria* (1907), Pierre Janet, a French doctor, described the major symptoms of hysteria as a pain or strange sensation in some part of the body, often below the stomach, which then spreads to an area just above the stomach, the chest, and the throat (choking).

24. During the Salem Witch Trials, Elizabeth Brown said that a specter in the form of a bird was pecking her legs, then her stomach, and then her throat.

25. John Locke, who lived in England in the 1600s and who was well known for his scholarly books, said that spirits (specters) could appear in the material world: "Spirits can assume to themselves bodies of different bulk, figure, and conformation of parts."

26. Thomas Hobbes, a famous political thinker in seventeenth-century England, wrote: "As for witches, I think not that their witchcraft is any real power; but yet they are justly punished, for their false belief they have that they can do such mischief...."

27. In Boston in 1688, Goodwife Glover was tried as a witch. Testimony showed that when Glover stuck pins into one of her dolls, one of the Goodwin children fell into fits and convulsions. She was overheard in her jail cell yelling at the devil for having abandoned her at her moment of need in the trial.

28. Abigail Hobbs said that George Burroughs had brought puppets to her, and thorns to stick into those puppets. She also said that she had caused a death by following his instructions.

29. According to one author, "convulsive ergotism" (the type that may have occurred in Salem Village) has occurred almost exclusively in areas where people suffered from a lack of vitamin A.

30. One author says that it is common for all members of a family to develop symptoms of convulsive ergotism during epidemics.

31. Residents of Salem Village lived in an area where fish and dairy products, both good sources of vitamin A, were common.

[Continued on next page.]

Salem Witch Hysteria: Glossary of Terms

A number of terms in this lesson might be unfamiliar to you or are used in a particular manner regarding the witchcraft trials. This glossary explains some of those terms; others are explained when they are used in the readings.

Afflicted To be distressed or tormented. In this lesson, it refers to those who appeared to be tormented by witchcraft.

Congregation The members of a particular church.

Devil's Book A book in which the devil was reported to keep a record of the souls he owned. A person who signed his or her name in this book indicated that he or she was now a witch.

Devil's Mark A mark on a witch's body where the devil or familiar sucked the blood of the witch, thereby feeding on her soul.

Examination A pretrial hearing to determine if there is enough evidence to try the accused in court. Similar to an indictment or Grand Jury hearing today.

Familiar A small animal, such as a cat or dog, that served as a messenger between the devil and the witch.

Goodwife (Goody) A title of address for married women; equivalent of Mrs.

Hysteria [1](medical) Physical ailments, such as pain, itching, or convulsions, caused by a mental state.

[2]A common use of the term is to describe a person who, due to some upsetting experience, screams or yells uncontrollably.

[3]The term is also used in this problem to describe a time of fear and irrationality among a large group of people ("mass hysteria").

Meeting House The place the town gathered for religious services, as well as political matters. Usually the largest building in a town.

Minister The religious leader (also called reverend, pastor, or clergyman) of the Puritan Church in a town or village.

Spectral Evidence Testimony that an accused witch's spirit or ghost appeared to the accuser, sometimes tormenting the accuser.

Theocracy Government ruled and/or controlled by a religion. Iran is a modern-day example.

Witch [1]As used in Puritan New England, a woman who had sold her soul to the devil, thereby becoming an enemy of the Christian church.

[2]A more general definition is someone who uses magic.

Wizard A male witch.

[Continued on next page.]

[Continued from previous page.]

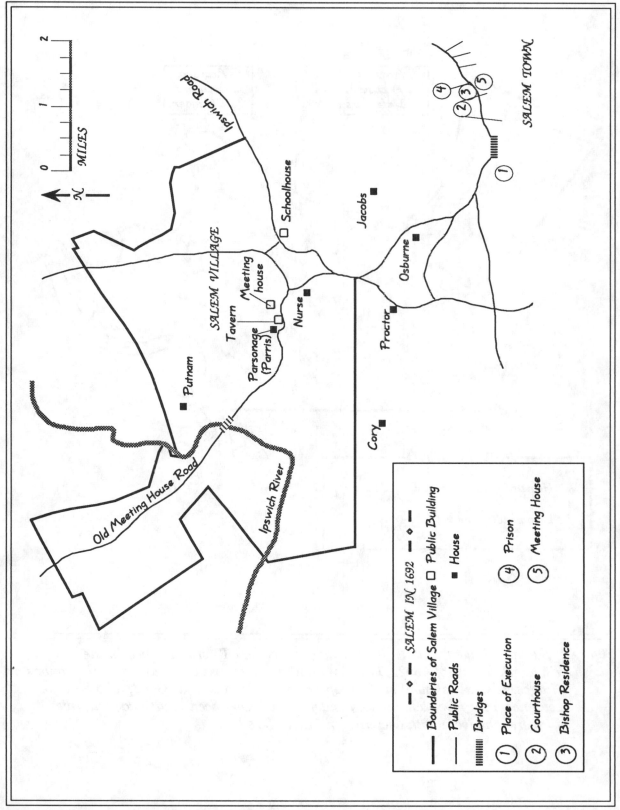

Figure 3: Salem and Salem Village in 1692, showing main roads and several locations important to the Witchcraft Trials

[Continued on next page.]

[Continued from previous page.]

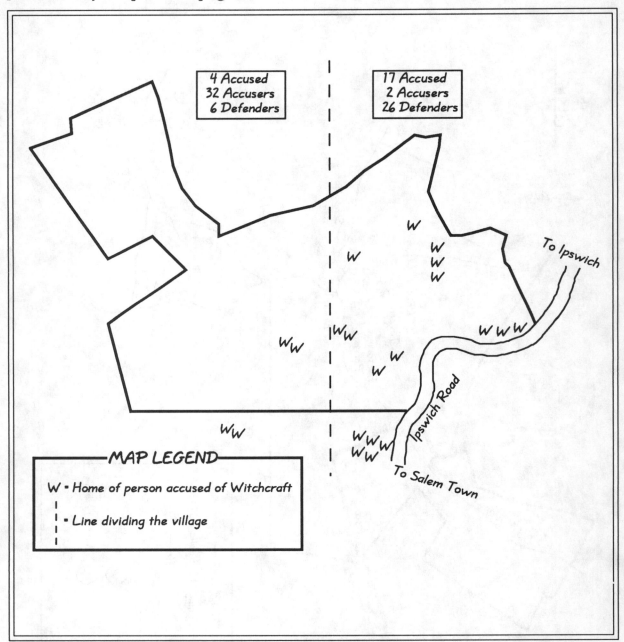

Figure 4: Salem Village residents (and some from Salem Town) involved in the
Witchcraft Trials of 1692. [This does not include those accused from other towns or
villages. Also not shown on the map are Sarah and Dorcas Good, who had no
residence; Mary DeRich, whose residence has never been identified; and five
villagers who were both accusers and defenders.]

[Continued on next page.]

Salem Witch Hysteria: Time Line of Events

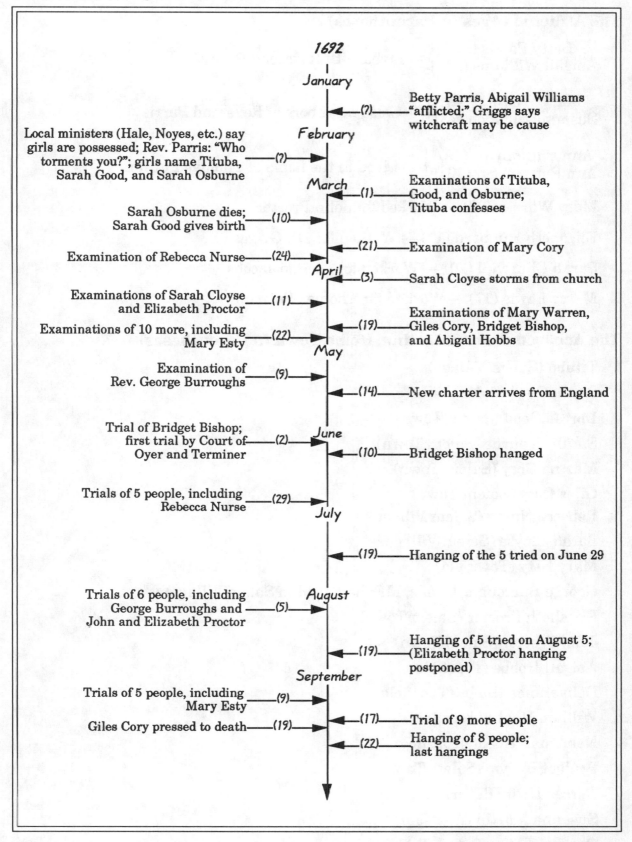

1692

January

(?) → Betty Parris, Abigail Williams "afflicted;" Griggs says witchcraft may be cause

February

Local ministers (Hale, Noyes, etc.) say girls are possessed; Rev. Parris: "Who torments you?"; girls name Tituba, Sarah Good, and Sarah Osburne → (?)

March

(1) → Examinations of Tituba, Good, and Osburne; Tituba confesses

Sarah Osburne dies; Sarah Good gives birth → (10)

(21) → Examination of Mary Cory

Examination of Rebecca Nurse → (24)

April

(3) → Sarah Cloyse storms from church

Examinations of Sarah Cloyse and Elizabeth Proctor → (11)

(19) → Examinations of Mary Warren, Giles Cory, Bridget Bishop, and Abigail Hobbs

Examinations of 10 more, including Mary Esty → (22)

May

Examination of Rev. George Burroughs → (9)

(14) → New charter arrives from England

Trial of Bridget Bishop; first trial by Court of Oyer and Terminer → (2) June

(10) → Bridget Bishop hanged

Trials of 5 people, including Rebecca Nurse → (29)

July

(19) → Hanging of the 5 tried on June 29

Trials of 6 people, including George Burroughs and John and Elizabeth Proctor → (5) August

(19) → Hanging of 5 tried on August 5; (Elizabeth Proctor hanging postponed)

September

Trials of 5 people, including Mary Esty → (9)

(17) → Trial of 9 more people

Giles Cory pressed to death → (19)

(22) → Hanging of 8 people; last hangings

[Continued on next page.]

Salem Witch Hysteria: The Afflicted and the Accused

The Afflicted (Ages in Parentheses)

Betty Parris (9)
Abigail Williams (11) } — Lived with Reverend Parris

Mary Wolcott (16)
Susanna Sheldon (18) } — Close neighbors of Reverend Parris

Ann Putnam Jr. (12)
Ann Putnam Sr. (30s) } — Lived in the home of Thomas Putnam

Mary Warren (20) — Worked for John Proctor

Elizabeth Hubbard (17) — Worked for Dr. Griggs

Sarah Churchill (20) — Worked for George Jacobs

Mercy Lewis (17) — Worked for Thomas Putnam

The Accused (Partial Listing; Home Town in Parentheses)

Tituba (Salem Village)

Sarah Good (Salem Village)

Dorcas Good (Salem Town)

Sarah Osburne (Salem Town)

Martha Cory (Salem Town)

Giles Cory (Salem Town)

Rebecca Nurse (Salem Village)

Sarah Cloyse (Salem Village)

Mary Esty (Topsfield)

George Burroughs (Wells, ME; had lived in Salem Village)

Elizabeth Proctor (Salem Town)

John Proctor (Salem Town)

Abigail Hobbs (Topsfield)

Deliverance Hobbs (Topsfield)

William Hobbs (Topsfield)

Nehemiah Abbot (Topsfield)

Bridget Bishop (Salem Town)

Dorcas Hoar (Beverly)

Susanna Martin (Amesbury)

George Jacobs (Salem Town)

[Continued on next page.]

Salem Witchcraft Trials: Interpretation A

(1) In Salem Village, Reverend Samuel Parris, like ministers in all colonial Massachusetts towns, was an important, well-respected person and a leader. In January 1692 the two girls who lived in his household, Betty Parris and Abigail Williams (his niece), became sick and began behaving oddly. News of the illness spread, and more girls seemed to become afflicted. Dr. Griggs, a local physician who was called in to examine Betty and Abigail, declared, "The evil hand is on them," meaning the girls were possessed by evil spirits.

(2) Since the cause of the disease was deemed a spiritual one, ministers had to deal with it. Reverend Parris called in half a dozen ministers from local towns, including Nicholas Noyes of Salem Town and John Hale of Beverly. But instead of trying to stop the girls' behavior, they inflamed it by asking, "Who is it who torments you?" Reverend Parris even started suggesting names. When he suggested the name of Tituba, who had done some fortune telling with the afflicted girls, Betty Parris repeated the name, thus suggesting that Tituba was afflicting them. The ministers had converted a minor incident into a full-blown hysteria. The witch hunt was on.

(3) Accused witches were arrested and taken to the meeting house for examination to see if the evidence against them was sufficient to have them tried in court. "Spectral evidence" was presented, with the afflicted girls saying that the spirit of the accused witch was hurting them.

(4) Some people questioned the use of such evidence; but each time doubts were raised, the ministers would rekindle the mad hysteria. For example, Reverend Deodat Lawson gave a sermon in March 1692 to the congregation in Salem Village in which he stressed that Satan could use apparently good Christians as witches.[1] This reassured people that the apparently devout Rebecca Nurse could, in fact, be a witch. On April 3 Reverend Parris preached, naming as his scripture, "Have I not chosen you twelve, and one of you is a devil?" Then Parris added, "Christ knows how many devils there are in His church, and who they are."[2]

(5) Ministers outside the local Salem area also spread the hysteria. The Reverend Joseph Ballard asked Ann Putnam, Jr., to come to Andover to see if Martha Carrier was causing his wife's illness, and the witch hysteria soon spread to Andover.[3]

(6) When a controversy arose among the judges concerning whether to allow spectral evidence, they asked the ministers for advice. The ministers advised them to be careful of such evidence, but to prosecute the accused witches vigorously.[4] Since a witch wasn't supposed to be able to say the Lord's Prayer, the crowd became very disturbed when George Burroughs said the Lord's Prayer just before he was to be hanged. The Reverend Cotton Mather reassured the crowd, saying that the devil was never more subtle than when he appeared as "an Angel of Light." Burroughs was hanged.[5]

(7) In short, ministers were responsible for starting the hysteria and for continuing it once it had begun. The result was the death of twenty innocent people. Although the reasons for the ministers' behavior are complex, a key factor was their drive to be in control. Puritan theocracy was declining, as shown by the 1692 charter brought back from England,[6] and the clergy was

[Continued on next page.]

Interpretation A
[Continued from previous page.]

losing its power. To reestablish their influence in the community, the ministers charged that the area was under attack by Satan. The common people were duly scared and turned to the ministers for guidance. The ministers' control could not last, however. Eventually many people, having seen the shedding of innocent blood, turned away from the rigid views of the clergy.

Endnotes for Interpretation A

1 Charles Upham, *Salem Witchcraft,* vol. 2 (Boston: Wiggins and Lunt, 1867; reprinted 1959), pp. 75-87. The entire sermon is quoted in this source.

2 Robert Calef, *More Wonders of the Invisible World, 1700* (London, 1700; reprinted Bainbridge, NY: York Mail-Press, 1972). Calef lived in Boston at the time of the trials. At one point his name was mentioned as a possible wizard, but he was never called to examination or trial.

3 Ibid. pp. 371–6.

4 Thomas Hutchinson, *History of the Colony and Province of Massachusetts Bay,* vol. 2, ed. Lawrence Shaw Mayo (Cambridge: Harvard University Press, 1936), pp. 38–9. This book contains reprints of some of the original sources regarding the trials, including this letter by the ministers.

5 Calef, *More Invisible World*, pp. 360–1. Calef may have been an eyewitness to this hanging.

6 The new charter, brought back in May 1692, allowed any propertied Christian male, not just Puritans, to vote. Also, the governor was to be appointed by the King, not elected by the people (that is, by the congregations of the Puritan churches).

Salem Witchcraft Trials: Interpretation B

(1) Winters in seventeenth-century New England were harsh, especially for females. Beginning in December, 1691, some of the girls in Salem Village, depressed by the lack of any legitimate outlet in Puritan society for their natural emotional energy and inflamed by the Puritan belief in sinfulness and evil, found relief for their tensions by starting a mass hysteria. The girls created the excitement and attention they craved, but twenty innocent people died as a result of their actions.

(2) The madness began in the home of the minister of Salem Village, Reverend Samuel Parris. During the winter months of 1691–1692, Betty Parris, Abigail Williams (Reverend Parris' niece), and six or seven neighbor girls gathered to listen to fortune-telling stories told by Parris's West Indian slave, Tituba. Betty Parris, probably because of the tales, became sick in January 1692. The other girls soon followed suit, exhibiting convulsions, screaming, and general fits. Adults in the area had never seen such behavior, and most really thought the girls were suffering. Since demon possession was an accepted cause for weird behavior and physical illness in seventeenth-century Massachusetts, it was natural to ask the girls who was afflicting them.

(3) The girls, of course, cooperated by naming their afflicters. Tituba, Sarah Good, and Sarah Osburne were accused and brought in for examination on the charge of witchcraft. Tituba confessed to save her neck and accused Sarah Good of also being a witch.[1] At

[Continued on next page.]

Interpretation B
[Continued from previous page.]

the examinations the girls' visions of the specters of the accused were taken as nearly foolproof evidence of guilt.[2] The girls were now among the most important people in the village.

(4) As the girls accused more people of witchcraft, and as more examinations and trials were held, the girls' importance rose still further. Several times the afflicted girls were able, through their actions, to reverse decisions that adults had made.

- When Mary Esty was released from jail, one afflicted girl, Mercy Lewis, fell deathly ill. The other afflicted girls said it was the specter of Mary Esty which was killing Mercy. Mary Esty was again arrested, and Mercy recovered.[3]

- When the jury found Rebecca Nurse "not guilty," the afflicted girls exploded into fits. The jury reconsidered the case, then returned a "guilty" verdict.[4]

(5) But the girls were also caught in the web of hysteria. Having captured the attention of the adult world, they could not easily back out. Arrests, examinations, and trials were very serious matters. It would not have been well-received had the girls said they had just been kidding.

(6) One girl, Mary Warren, did say that she—as well as the other afflicted girls—was wrong in her accusations.

The others promptly accused her of becoming a witch, and Mary decided to join the afflicted girls once more.[5] Another accuser, Sarah Churchill, said that her accusations against George Jacobs were also a lie. The court did not believe her, however, and she too was restored to the accusers' ranks.[6]

(7) So the madness continued. Accused witches, some having been beaten or tortured, confessed to their crimes and implicated other people. The hysteria spread until the jails were filled with over 150 accused witches. Finally, the voice of reason returned to the area, and the hysteria died down.

(8) Interestingly, the girls had no recurrence of convulsions or fits when the madness ended and the "witches" were returned to society. With adults no longer paying special attention to them, the girls had no reason to act strangely.

(9) The girls of Salem Village brought on the witch hunt when they noticed that their apparent afflictions brought them a great deal of attention from the adult world. Many adults, especially those with problems of mental illness (such as Ann Putnam, Sr.),[7] were also caught up in the unreal world of hysteria, joining the afflicted girls and testifying against each other. The girls created this nightmarish world, then could not stop it. Unfortunately, twenty people died before it ran its course.

Endnotes for Interpretation B

[1] Essex County (Massachusetts) Archives, *Salem Witchcraft, 1692*, vol. 1. [Report by Ezekial Cheever, secretary for this examination], p. 6.

[2] Hutchinson, *History of Massachusetts*, pp. 21–23. For example, the girls claimed they saw the devil whispering in Goody Cloyse's ear at her examination. At Martha Cory's examination, Ann Putnam, Jr., one of the afflicted girls, said she saw Cory's specter in the rafters.

[3] Essex County Archives, *Salem Witchcraft*, vol. 1, p. 117.

[4] Calef, "More Invisible World," pp. 358–60.

[5] Essex County Archives, *Salem Witchcraft*, vol. 1, pp. 29–31.

[Continued on next page.]

Endnotes for Interpretation B
[Continued from previous page.]

[6] Elliot W. Woodward, *Records of the Salem Witchcraft Trials*, vol. 1 (Roxbury, MA: W. Elliot Woodward, 1864; reprinted New York: DaCapo Press, 1969), p. 14. [Reprinted manuscript documents from the trials.]

[7] Upham, *Salem Witchcraft*, vol. 2, pp. 253 ff. (and following).

Salem Witchcraft Trials: Interpretation C

(1) The fantastic events of Salem Village in 1692 seem to defy rational explanation. Historians have dismissed a large part of the trial evidence as imaginary, yet the testimony suggests that there was a rational cause for the hysteria: rye bread. Many of the descriptions of visions seen by the young girls, along with their disorderly speech, odd gestures, and convulsions are symptoms of "convulsive ergot poisoning"—caused by eating rye bread which contains the ergot fungus.

(2) First of all, the time of year fits the timing for ergot poisoning. The rye was harvested around Thanksgiving for the winter and spring. The children's symptoms first appeared in December 1691 and continued through the spring of 1692. There is no further mention of anyone being afflicted the next year, probably because only the one harvest was infected.

(3) Secondly, women (especially pregnant women) and children have been more susceptible to the disease in some epidemics. For example, 56 percent in one epidemic were under ten years of age, and 60 percent in another were under the age of fifteen. Most of those afflicted in 1692 in Salem Village were teenaged females.

(4) According to tree rings in eastern New England, the growing seasons of 1690, 1691, and 1692 were cooler than normal.[1] Furthermore, people in Boston wrote in their diaries that the winters of 1690–1691 and 1691–1692 were very cold.[2] These conditions are ideal for ergot fungus growth.

(5) A closer look at the afflicted girls reveals even more evidence favoring the ergot theory. Three of the afflicted lived in the Putnam residence. A large part of the Putnam land was swampy meadows, an ideal location for ergot in great abundance. It is highly likely that the rye the Putnams grew was infected. Two of the other afflicted girls were in the household of the Reverend Parris. Two-thirds of Parris's salary was paid in provisions and, since Putnam was the largest landholder and an avid supporter of Reverend Parris, it seems reasonable to conclude that a good deal of the rye he received came from the Putnams' fields.

(6) Another of the afflicted girls, Elizabeth Hubbard, was a servant in the home of Dr. Griggs. As the town's only doctor, Dr. Griggs would probably have had many occasions to treat the often-sick Ann Putnam, Sr. Since doctors were usually paid in provisions, Dr. Griggs would probably have had some Putnam rye. All twenty-two of the afflicted people in Salem Village lived in households located on or at the edge of soils ideally suited to rye cultivation: moist, acid, sandy loam.

(7) The symptoms the afflicted girls complained of are symptoms of ergot poisoning. Choking is a sign of the disease's effect on the involuntary muscle fibers. Biting, pinching, and pricking sensations, of which the afflicted complained, may allude to the under-the-skin crawling, tingling sensation experienced by ergotism victims. Vomiting

[Continued on next page.]

Interpretation C

[Continued from previous page.]

and bowel difficulties are also symptoms of ergotism.[3]

(8) The visions of specters—seen by the afflicted, but no one else—had all the characteristics of hallucinations brought on by lysergic acid diethylamide (LSD), of which ergot is the source. It should be noted that several people who reported these visions were otherwise reliable, respectable people.

(9) Ergot poisoning can be a serious health problem, in some cases resulting in death. In Fairfield, Connecticut, in 1692, several people complained of symptoms similar to those in Salem Village. Two afflicted persons died.[4] No one can explain this away as faking or spite against neighbors; it was likely to have been ergot poisoning.

(10) Although several theories have been advanced to show why the adults acted the way they did in the Witch Hysteria of 1692, no theory has adequately explained why the girls became afflicted in the first place. The weather, the crops grown, and the symptoms complained of by the afflicted all lead to the conclusion that rye bread was the demon that possessed Salem Village in 1692.

Endnotes for Interpretation C

[1] E. DeWitt and M. Ames, eds., *Tree Ring Chronology of Eastern North America* (Tucson: University of Arizona Press, 1978). The width of a tree ring gives a clue to the average temperature for that year. The tree rings for 1690, 1691, and 1692 are narrower, indicating less tree growth and, by implication, lower average temperatures.

[2] "Diary of Lawrence Hammond, 1891-92," *Proceedings of the Massachusetts Historical Society,* 7:160.

[3] B. Berde and H.O. Schild, eds., *Ergot Alkaloids and Related Compounds* (New York: Springer, 1987).

[4] J. M. Taylor, *The Witchcraft Delusion in Colonial Connecticut, 1647–1697* (Stratford, CT: J. E. Edwards, 1908). In addition, seven infants in the Salem area either developed or died of symptoms of ergot poisoning.

Salem Witchcraft Trials: Interpretation D

(1) Other historians are wrong in how they have viewed the Salem Witch Trials of 1692. They assume: (a) no witchcraft was practiced in Salem; (b) the girls lied when accusing other people; (c) the ministers caused the Trials by whipping the people into "mass hysteria" with their sermons. The facts show that these common assumptions are wrong.

(2) First, witchcraft *was* practiced in Salem, as it was throughout the world in 1692. About fifty people in the Salem Trials confessed to being witches.

Tituba, the slave who probably started the girls going crazy and accusing other people of witchcraft, confessed to being a witch. She said that the devil had come to her in the shape of a man—a tall man with white hair and dressed in black. This man had shown her a book, and she had made a mark in it, a mark that was "red like blood." Sometimes the man in black had brought four witches with him—Sarah Good, Sarah Osburn, and two women from Boston whose names she did not know—and

[Continued on next page.]

Interpretation D

[Continued from previous page.]

they had forced her to go with them to afflict the girls.[1]

(3) Bridget Bishop was another person in Salem who practiced witchcraft. Many Village people believed she did, and two men testified in court that they found several puppets made of rags and hogs' bristles in a house where she had lived.[2] The puppets had headless pins in them with the points sticking outward. This was a common witchcraft procedure in the 1600s. Bridget Bishop could make no reasonable reply to these court charges. The slave Candy also confessed to being a witch and brought her puppets to court when asked how she afflicted the girls.[3]

(4) At least six people testified that Margaret Rule, who was afflicted in 1693, was lifted from her bed "by an invisible force" so that none of her body rested either on the bed or on any other support.[4] That is, she levitated, which could be viewed as a sign of supernatural power.

(5) Thus, there is no question that witchcraft was practiced in the Salem of 1692. More importantly, almost everyone in Salem, and in the world at that time, believed in witchcraft. People who believe in witchcraft can be afflicted by it.

(6) Second, although some of the girls may have lied in accusing other people, most of them did not. The girls were actually hysterical, in the medical sense of that term. ("Hysterical" means that a person is in a mental state of mind which causes certain symptoms, like pain or convulsions. People really suffer from the pain, but because of their mental, rather than their physical, state.)

(7) Witnesses repeatedly said that the girls' fits were so grotesque and so violent that they could not possibly have been acting. For example, the Reverend John Hale of Beverly wrote, "Their arms, necks, and backs were turned this way and that way so as it was impossible for them to do of themselves, and beyond the power of any epileptic fits, or natural disease to effect."[5] Moreover, the girls' symptoms were the same as those identified by psychologists as typical for hysterics; for example, pain in the legs, then in other organs, then choking.

(8) Third, the ministers, rather than whipping the people into a "mass hysteria" which then led to the Trials, tried to control the Trials from the beginning. It is well to remember that the Trials were held by governmental authorities, not by ministers. Before anyone had been executed, Cotton Mather, a leading Massachusetts clergyman, suggested that the afflicted people be cured by prayer and requested that the court be very careful about allowing spectral evidence, so that no innocent people would be executed.[6] Later, a letter from several Boston ministers questioned the evidence used by the court to convict people.

(9) It is clear that historians have been wrong in their views of the Salem Witch Trials of 1692. First, the evidence shows that witchcraft really was practiced in Salem and it really affected people. Second, the girls did not lie in accusing others; but rather they were medically hysterical and actually thought they were being attacked by witches. Third, the ministers, far from causing the Trials, tried to correct the abuses of the Trials.

(10) This new evidence helps us understand the Salem Witchcraft Trials as they really were.

[Continued on next page.]

Endnotes for Interpretation D

[Continued from previous page.]

[1] Woodward, *Records*, pp. 6–8.

[2] Cotton Mather, *The Wonders of the Invisible World* (London: John Russell Smith, 1862), reprinted in *Narratives of the Witchcraft Cases, 1648–1706*, ed. G. L. Burr (New York: Scribners, 1914), p. 228. Mather is not an objective observer, but a comparison of his account to the trial records shows him to be very accurate in recording facts.

[3] Ibid., pp. 215–22. Rev. George Burroughs also had a reputation for the occult. He tricked his wife and brother-in-law into thinking he knew of one of their conversations by reading their minds through occult supernatural powers, although he may have been eavesdropping. He said, "My God makes known your thoughts to me." Both his wife and brother-in-law understood from this that his god was the devil, since the Christian God doesn't deal in occult powers about family gossip, but the devil does. Rev. Burroughs also was caught lying at his trial, and he hadn't taken communion for a long time.

[4] Calef, *More Invisible World*. Cotton Mather obtained signed confirmations of this and other instances of levitation. Also, Sarah Good, when requested by Rev. Noyes at her execution to confess to being a witch, replied, "I am no more a witch than you are a wizard. If you take my life away, God will give you blood to drink." She was executed. Tradition has it that when Noyes lay dying twenty-five years later, he did, indeed, choke on blood in his mouth.

[5] George Lyman Kittredge, *Witchcraft in Old and New England* (Cambridge: Harvard University Press, 1929), p. 338. As another example, Mary Warren was reported on September 2 as having "a pin run through her hand and blood running out of her mouth." [Recorded in Woodward, ed., *Salem Witchcraft*, vol. 2, p. 155.]

[6] Cotton Mather to Judge John Richards, May 1692, Massachusetts Historical Society Collections, 4th series, vol. 8, pp. 391–7.

Salem Witchcraft Trials: Interpretation E

(1) Until now, historians of the Salem witch hysteria of 1692 have focused on why the girls originally accused others of witchcraft. This focus on the girls has drawn attention away from a much more important question, which is why the adults listened to the girls. It was the parents who could have squashed it, but it was the parents who listened to, and even encouraged, it. Indeed, it was adults who first asked, "Who is it that afflicts you?" Only at this point did the girls begin to accuse people.

(2) There were some important psychological reasons for people in Salem Village to lash out at others. It wasn't that the accusers consciously used the Trials to get even with their enemies; it was more that they saw in the accusations an explanation for why things were not working out the way they wanted. They were not reluctant to believe that their enemies were allied with the devil; it gave them a reason for their feelings.

(3) It is toward Salem Village, then, that study should be directed. If divisions within the village were the main cause of the witch hysteria, accusers and defenders of the witches should be on opposing sides of issues. By examining divisions within the village, an understanding of the hysteria may be gained.

(4) The main issue dividing the people of Salem Village was whether its government should be independent from Salem Town. Salem Village of the 1690s was mainly agricultural; Salem Town was becoming more commerce-centered and more dominated by merchants.

(5) Farmers in Salem Village who did not trade much with Salem Town

[Continued on next page.]

Interpretation E

[Continued from previous page.]

gained little from being part of the Town; worse, they had to pay Town taxes. This problem was especially bothersome for farmers in the northwest section of the Village, which was remote from Salem Town. These farmers saw increased commercialization in Salem Town as a symbol of commercialization within their whole society, something the Bible warned against.

(6) These farmers, pressing hard for independence from Salem Town, were opposed by a second group. This opposing group, composed of farmers who sold their crops through Salem Town and merchants who lived along the Ipswich Road, had many contacts with people from the Town. Since this group gained by the Village's contact with the Town, they opposed separation.

(7) The central issue in the struggle over independence for the Village was the Church. Those who favored a separate government for the Village also favored a separate church and a separate, ordained minister. Again, they were opposed by the group who wanted to stay as part of the Town. The Village had achieved a somewhat independent church in the 1670s, but this led to numerous disputes over the next twenty years.

(8) Several petitions, some in opposition to the ministers, others supporting them, were sent to the Massachusetts legislature (called the General Court). In 1689 Reverend Samuel Parris was ordained, giving the Salem Village Church its independence.[1] Opposition arose again against the new minister,[2] and at this difficult point the witch accusations of 1692 began.

(9) The pattern of accuser and accused shows very well how divisions within the Village help account for the hysteria. Almost all accusers lived in the western part of the Village, more remote from Salem Town; most defenders lived in the eastern part of the village, closer to Ipswich Road and to Salem Town.[3] Most accusers later signed a petition supporting Reverend Parris; defenders mostly signed a petition opposing him.[4] Accusers were, on a whole, from the middle and lower classes; defenders tended to be more prosperous. (Almost all of the richest families in the village were defenders.)

(10) It is important to note that two of the afflicted girls were from Reverend Parris's own household—one his daughter, the other his niece. Three of the other afflicted females were from the household of Thomas Putnam, Jr. Although Putnam was from a wealthy family, he opposed close ties with Salem Town, possibly because his family felt they had been cheated of their rightful inheritance by his father's second wife, Mary Veren of Salem Town, and Israel Porter, a villager who supported closer ties with Salem Town.

(11) These patterns show that the accusers had real motives, stemming from divisions within Salem Village, to attack certain people. This does not, however, entirely explain what transpired in 1692, since many leaders of the anti-Parris group were not accused of witchcraft. It seems that the girls accused whomever they decided to accuse. Adults in the pro-Parris group, however, encouraged the accusations because most of the accused were in the anti-Parris group.

(12) Another factor which must be considered is that, of the 142 persons named as witches in 1692, 82 percent lived outside Salem Village. This sug-

[Continued on next page.]

Interpretation E

[Continued from previous page.]

gests that the people of Salem Village were striking out at external forces—forces of commercialization and evil which threatened, and indeed were changing, their village life. Reverend Parris identified those forces in a sermon in 1690 as a "lamentable harmony between wicked men and devils, in their opposition of God's kingdom and interests."[5]

(13) Because the people of Salem Village felt drawn away from their pure religion by a commercial orientation, they felt guilty. In their guilt and efforts to resist change, they fueled the flames of the witch hysteria of 1692.

Endnotes for Interpretation E

[1] Ordination of a minister to lead a village church gave that church recognition of independence.

[2] Some people in the village did not pay their taxes to support the minister. They objected to the terms under which Reverend Parris was hired and disputed the villagers' obligation to take Reverend Parris firewood.

[3] See Figure 4, page 48.

[4] Information on pro-Parris and anti-Parris petitions are from church records, following the entry for April 3, 1695. Data on accusers and defenders are from "Verbatim Transcripts of Salem Witchcraft Papers," compiled under the supervision of Archie N. Frost, Salem Clerk of Courts (1938). Of the twenty-seven who supported the Witchcraft Trials by testifying against one or more of the accused witches, twenty-one later (in 1695) signed the pro-Parris petition; six signed the anti-Parris petition. Of the twenty who registered their opposition to the trials, one signed the pro-Parris petition; nineteen signed the anti-Parris petition.

[5] Reverend Samuel Parris, *Sermon Book,* January 12, 1690.

Interpretation F

The causes of the Salem witch hysteria of 1692 are difficult to figure out. A clue, however, is provided by a look at the persons accused. Tituba was a slave; Sarah Osborne was a bedridden old women; Sarah Good was a beggar who didn't get along well with other people. All of these people were outcasts from society. They were easy to pick on. Society gained from the trials by showing the limits of antisocial or deviant behavior. Therefore, the trials were probably attempts to control social behavior and insure conformity.

Interpretation G

(1) Many historians have focused on the reasons for the original outbreak of the witch hysteria of 1692 and on the conditions in the society which inflamed it. Why 1692? Why then, in a society which had believed in witchcraft all along?

(2) A look at conditions in 1692 shows that many factors caused instability at the time. There was Bacon's Rebellion in Virginia, Leisler's Rebellion in New York, and a Protestant revolt in Maryland. Puritanism was declining
[Continued on next page.]

Interpretation G

[Continued from previous page.]

in Massachusetts. People feared God's wrath and the possibility of resulting inroads by the devil's agents. This was compounded by the fact that the colony lost its charter in 1684, with a royal governor, Sir Edmond Andros, coming to rule Massachusetts, along with the rest of New England.

(3) With the outbreak of civil war in England in 1688, the people of Boston threw Andros out of office and into jail. The colony did not receive a new charter until 1692. Throughout this period the colony had an air of tentativeness and indecision in political affairs. Besides the political and religious unrest, the colony in 1691–1692 was torn by a great number of arguments, the threat of Indian attack, war with the French, high taxes, a severe winter, threats of smallpox, and local disagreements over land claims.

(4) Collectively, these many unstable conditions are the reasons why the original accusations in Salem Village ended in a full-scale hysteria and witch hunt. The situation was so tense that, when there was a spark, it exploded.

LESSON 11   Evaluating Evidence: Strengths and Weaknesses

Q Each item below contains a question followed by two samples of evidence. Put a check (√) on the line next to the stronger piece of evidence and explain your answer in the space below the item. If you need help, refer to the section on **Evidence** in the "Guide to Critical Thinking" (Unit 1).

1. If you wanted to determine whether you should believe Philip's story, which argument presents the stronger evidence?

    ____ Philip (to the teacher): "I did my homework, but I lost it on the way to school. It fell out of my book into a sewer drain."

    ____ Philip (to the teacher): "I couldn't do my homework last night because I had to go with my parents to a wedding."

    Explain your choice.

2. If you wanted to know what the Proclamation of 1763 allowed and prevented, which source would provide better evidence?

    ____ A reprint of the Proclamation of 1763.

    ____ A book about the causes of the American Revolution.

    Explain your choice.

3. If you wanted to know whether British customs officers were unfairly enforcing the customs laws so they could make money, which source would be considered better evidence?

    ____ In a letter to a friend, a British customs officer wrote that he made a great deal of money by catching colonists for breaking customs laws they couldn't obey.

    ____ A colonial merchant told a fellow colonist that British customs officers were unfair in their enforcement of the customs laws.

    Explain your choice.

[Continued on next page.]

[Continued from previous page.]

4. If you wanted to determine whether British General Sir Jeffrey Amherst incited (pushed) the Indians into war by his foolish policies, which would be the better evidence?

    ____ A colonist says that Amherst's policies—especially those of building blockhouses on the lands of friendly Indians and of giving no gifts to the Indians—are ridiculous.

    ____ The Indian chief Pontiac said he started the war because Amherst's policies were very unfair to the Indians.

    Explain your choice.

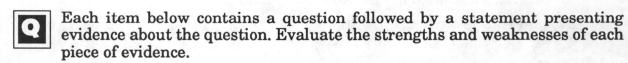 Each item below contains a question followed by a statement presenting evidence about the question. Evaluate the strengths and weaknesses of each piece of evidence.

5. Did some colonial governors make money from corrupt collection of customs duties?

    Some governors used corruption in customs collections to add to their income. Governor Bernard of Massachusetts was especially notorious [well-known for bad reasons] in this respect; Mr. Temple, the Surveyor General of the Customs (a British official who kept records of customs' collections), estimated that the governor received more from the customs corruption than from his regular salary.[1]

6. What was the British government trying to achieve when it passed the Intolerable Acts?

    The British government was very upset by the defiance shown by the colonists in the Boston Tea Party. Parliament passed the Intolerable Acts to show a strong policy by the British government. It was designed to isolate and punish one colony—Massachusetts.

_____

[1] Oliver Dickerson, *The Navigation Acts and the American Revolution* (Philadelphia: University of Pennsylvania Press, 1963), p. 85.

LESSON 12   Identifying and Evaluating
Comparison Arguments

Q Identify the arguments or claims that use comparison reasoning by putting a
C on the line in front of those arguments. If you need help, refer to the
section on **Comparisons** in the "Guide to Critical Thinking" (Unit 1).

_____ 1. The clock stopped because the batteries went dead.

_____ 2. Helen has been running over thirty miles per week, which is why she is
now a better runner than Ruth.

_____ 3. Unemployment is lower this year than last year, so the economy must be
improving.

_____ 4. The Boston Massacre, like the Kent State shootings some two hundred
years later, had the effect of increasing opposition to the government and
its policies.

_____ 5. The American colonists who destroyed the tea at the Boston Tea Party
were wrong. It is never right to destroy property, even in protest.

Q Evaluate the following comparison arguments.

6. George has definitely improved his piano playing. Last year he had difficulty
playing the simplest tunes. Now he plays complicated pieces without making
any mistakes.

a. What two cases are being compared?
Case A:

Case B:

b. Is this a comparison of similarity or of difference?

c. What similarities or differences are there between the two cases?

d. Could factors other than the difficulty of the tunes have been compared?
If so, what are they?

e. How strong is the comparison?

[Continued on next page.]

[Continued from previous page.]

7. Some people have claimed that the American colonies revolted against England partly because of the trade restrictions England placed upon them in the Navigation Acts. For example, under the Navigation Acts some goods had to be shipped through England first, before they could be shipped to other countries; other goods could be sold only to England.

    This view is wrong, however, for although the Navigation Acts did place restrictions on the colonists, all in all the colonists benefitted. Statistics prove the point. In the early 1770s (under the Navigation Acts) the colonists exported about 100 million pounds of tobacco per year, but in 1810 (without the Navigation Acts) tobacco exports had dropped by 51.5 million pounds per year. It seems clear that without British help, especially in financing and marketing tobacco, Americans couldn't export as much.

    a. What two cases are being compared?

        Case A:

        Case B:

    b. Is this a comparison of similarity or of difference?

    c. What similarities or differences are there between the two cases?

    d. Could other factors or dates have been compared? If yes, which ones?

    e. How strong is the comparison?

© 1990 MIDWEST PUBLICATIONS, P.O. Box 448, Pacific Grove, CA 93950

LESSON 13   Evaluating and Making Generalizations

Q Evaluate the following generalizations. If you need help, refer to the section on **Generalizations** in the "Guide to Critical Thinking" (Unit 1). Use Figure 5 (below) to help you visualize the generalization for each item.

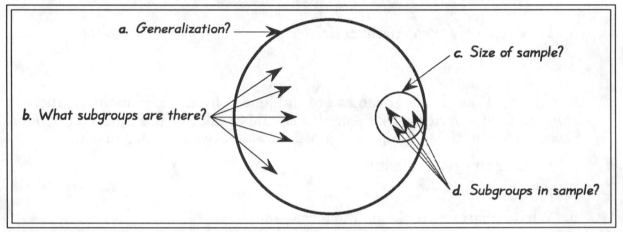

Figure 5: Relationship of generalizations, subgroups, and samples.

1. The colonists hated the Tea Act, as shown by their response to it. They showed their anger by the Boston Tea Party. In New York and in Philadelphia, the colonists wouldn't permit the tea to be taken off the ships. Only in Charleston was the tea landed, but even there it wasn't sold.
    a. What is the generalization?

    b. What subgroups make up the large group?

    c. How large is the sample?

    d. Does the sample have all the same subgroups?

    e. How strong is the generalization?

2. Most colonists were opposed to the Stamp Act. They boycotted British goods and formed the Stamp Act Congress, made up of representatives from nine of the thirteen colonies, to protest the tax.
    a. What is the generalization?

[Continued on next page.]

[Continued from previous page.]

(2.) b. What subgroups make up the large group?

c. How large is the sample?

d. Does the sample have all the same subgroups?

e. How strong is the generalization?

3. A majority of adult Americans were influenced by the argument of Thomas Paine in *Common Sense* that America should break free of England. *Common Sense* sold over 100,000 copies in a population of two million Americans.

a. What is the generalization?

b. What subgroups make up the large group?

c. How large is the sample?

d. Does the sample have all the same subgroups?

e. How strong is the generalization?

4. The American Revolution brought freedom and political equality for all Americans by allowing them to run their own government.

a. What is the generalization?

b. What subgroups make up the large group?

c. How large is the sample? (Hint: Who gets to run the new government?)

d. Does the sample have all the same subgroups?

e. How strong is the generalization?

[Continued on next page.]

 © 1990 MIDWEST PUBLICATIONS, P.O. Box 448, Pacific Grove, CA 93950

[Continued from previous page.]

 Write the letter of the most reasonable generalization on the line in front of item 5, then explain your choice in the space below.

_____ 5. Suppose you knew that in both the American and the French Revolutions the government backed down to the revolutionists, which only made the situation worse (i.e., more revolutionary). How far could you reasonably generalize this information?

    A. It's always wrong for a government to give in to demands.

    B. In a revolutionary situation, compromise by the government is always seen as a sign of weakness.

    C. In revolutions in the 1700s, compromise by the government was always seen as a sign of weakness.

Explain your choice.

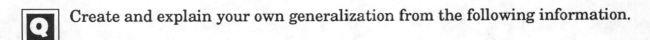

 Create and explain your own generalization from the following information.

6. Suppose you knew that guerrilla warfare tactics were important to winning the American Revolution. How far could you reasonably generalize this information? Write out your answer and explain your choice.

LESSON 14   Identifying Unstated Assumptions

Q Identify the unstated assumption(s) in each of the following items. If you need help, refer to the section on **Assumptions** in the "Guide to Critical Thinking" (Unit 1).

1. I can't find any sources in the school library for my research paper on the Stamp Act, so tonight I'm going to the public library to get some.

2. Phil must have gone home. I have looked in every room in the building, and he's not here.

3. Colonial smugglers must be tried by British judges in vice-admiralty courts. We certainly can't let them be tried in courts with juries of fellow colonists.

4. "British Soldiers Shoot Colonists in Bloody Massacre" [Newspaper headline, March, 1770]

5. The British have no right to prevent colonists from settling west of the Appalachian Mountains. The colonists have already begun to set up farms and towns there.

6. George Washington was a great leader who helped America win and preserve independence as a nation. His size and stature (height and appearance) helped him as a leader. He was six feet two inches tall, and his face appeared to be chiseled from granite.

LESSON 15   What Caused the American Revolution?

Background Information

The American Revolution is important to Americans because it gave birth to our nation. Most historians agree that the Revolutionary period began in 1763 with the end of the French and Indian War. Studies of the events leading to the Revolution refer to such causes as: the results of the French and Indian War, the Proclamation of 1763, the Sugar Act, the Townshend Duties, the Boston Massacre, the Boston Tea Party, the battles of Lexington and Concord, the pamphlet *Common Sense*, and the Declaration of Independence.

This lesson presents three historians' interpretations of the main causes of the American Revolution. Each historian refers to some of the events listed above, weaving those events into the particular pattern which comprises his or her interpretation of why the Revolution occurred. Dates in parentheses in the titles refer to when the interpretations were originally published.

The American Revolution: Historian A (1950)

(1) A number of causes have been proposed for the American Revolution. Some say it was a struggle for democratic rights; others see economic conflict as the key. Historians have failed, however, to examine the view from the British side. Looking at the causes of the American Revolution in the context of the whole British Empire, it becomes clear that the main cause of the Revolution was the French and Indian War or, more properly, the Great War for Empire.

(2) The colonial system in America worked reasonably well until 1754, when the French and Indian War broke out. By the end of the war in 1763, the system had been changed, the equilibrium shattered. The British, despite heavy taxes during the war, had a staggering national debt of £140 million—twice what it had been in 1754. They saw no alternative but to tax the colonists to pay off that debt. After all, British citizens were paying about twenty times more taxes than Americans.

(3) To further complicate the matter, British expenses increased as they faced the cost of paying the 10,000 troops needed to defend the expanded Empire they had gained from the French in the war. Colonists, the British government reasoned, should help pay for their own defense.

(4) The Proclamation of 1763 forbade colonists from settling west of the Appalachian Mountains. Other historians have represented this as a restriction on colonial freedom, a blunder by the British, or an attempt to help the British fur-trading interests. Actually, the Proclamation was another direct result of the French and Indian War. During the war against the French, the British needed Indian allies. To accomplish this end, they promised the land west of the mountains to the Ohio Valley Indians and other cooperating tribes. Thus, the Proclamation of 1763 was simply an extension of a promise made during the Great War.

[Continued on next page.]

Historian A (1950)
[Continued from previous page.]

(5)   Taxes were the inevitable result of the enormous British debt from the French and Indian War. The Stamp Act of 1765 came to symbolize both British tyranny and colonial protest. The protest, however, was no more defiant than those that colonists had made before 1754 against other British trade acts. What made the situation in 1765 so different that it led to Revolution? The answer is that the colonial-motherland relationship with the debt-ridden British no longer offered any advantage to the now geographically secure, prosperous, self-reliant colonists.

(6)   Had the French decisively won the Great War for the Empire, colonists would have needed British protection against the French threat. Without this threat, however, the colonies had no reason for accepting new British policies and taxes. Governor Thomas Hutchinson of Massachusetts wrote in 1773 to a British leader, "Before the peace [of 1773], I thought nothing so much to be desired as the cession (giving to England) of Canada [from France]. I am now convinced that if it had remained to the French, none of the spirit of opposition to the Mother Country would have yet appeared...." After the French and Indian War, the advantages of Empire were no longer mutual. The result was the American Revolution.

The American Revolution: Historian B (1967)

(1)   The leaders of the American Revolution wrote a lot, presenting their viewpoints and arguments in newspapers, letters, speeches, broadsides (single printed sheets that were passed around or posted on walls), and especially pamphlets. A pamphlet was a ten- to fifty-page (5,000–25,000 words) booklet, selling for a shilling or two, that expressed the opinion of the writer. From 1750 to 1776, four hundred pamphlets bearing on the causes of the Revolution were printed in America.[1] They were widely read, particularly by lawyers, ministers, merchants, and planters. A study of these pamphlets shows that colonial ideology (beliefs colonists held about the world) was the main cause of the American Revolution.

(2)   Two factors influenced the beliefs of colonists. First was the set of ideas they had brought with them from Europe, especially from England. Religious doctrine, the writings of the Enlightenment and, most importantly, of the English Civil War,[2] led to colonial beliefs that each person was sacred and endowed (supplied) with natural rights, that liberty was precious and could be snuffed out by the power of armies or governments, and that only a balance of governmental power among legislature, king, and courts could prevent the destruction of liberty.

(3)   The second, and more important, factor which influenced colonial ideology was the frontier. Colonists changed as they struggled with the vast American wilderness. They began to believe in the simple, virtuous life and that problems had to be resolved by the local community of ordinary citizens; the central government could not really understand their local concerns. Colonists thought that people became corrupt when they got away from the simple values of hard work

[Continued on next page.]

Historian B (1967)

[Continued from previous page.]

and honesty. Since corruption led to abuse of power, corruption was the biggest threat to liberty. The colonists saw an important lesson in the classical writings on ancient Rome that described the change in Roman society away from simple virtue, hard work, and public service toward corruption and decline. These popular writings were widely discussed in the colonies.[3]

(4) Through the lens of this ideology, colonists began to see a conspiracy to destroy their liberty in British policies of the 1760s and 1770s. The Stamp Act not only expanded government's power to tax individuals, it taxed them without the consent of their local representatives. The small amount of the tax showed even more dramatically the ideological, rather than economic, nature of the issue. The ultimate threat was to liberty, not to the pocketbook.[4]

(5) Later British policies provided further proof of the conspiracy against colonial liberty. New customs officials were appointed under the Townshend Act. Colonists regarded these officials as corrupt agents who, to fill their own pockets, trapped colonial merchants on legal technicalities. One-judge admiralty (Navy) courts, with judges frequently appointed by royal governors as reward for political favors, replaced the trial-by-jury colonial courts.[5] Writs of assistance (general search warrants) allowed government officials to search an individual's home for any type of goods. Appointed governors moved or dissolved (ended) colonial legislatures. Worst of all, British troops—standing armies— were stationed in the colonies. The Boston Massacre removed all doubts about why these troops were present; they were there to terrify the colonial population into obeying British policies.[6]

(6) The key issue to the colonists was the extent of Parliament's control over them. When Parliament passed the Declaratory Act, it asserted complete sovereignty (power to rule) over the colonists. This stated that Parliament had authority to make laws to bind (rule) the people of America "in all cases whatsoever." The colonists felt their only choice was between independence and slavery to the British government. Since colonists did not want to give up the liberty they, in practice, already enjoyed, they chose independence.

(7) The Declaration of Independence illustrated (showed) the Americans' concern for these ideological issues related to their liberty. In it, colonists charged the King with dissolving colonial legislatures, making judges dependent upon him for their jobs and salaries, sending swarms of officials to harass (bother) the colonists, keeping standing armies in the colonies during peacetime, and imposing taxes without colonial consent. These charges, far from being propaganda, were real issues to the signers of the Declaration.

(8) These ideological issues which led to the American Revolution helped shape the government of the new nation. Local control of government, civilian authority over the military, protection against unreasonable search and seizure, trial by jury, checks and balances within government, and the idea of limited power as demonstrated in the federal system of government all grew from the ideological struggles of the colonists against the British up to 1776.

Endnotes for Historian B

[1] I [Historian B] studied the pamphlets for several years and counted this number concerning the Anglo-American controversy. *[Continued on next page.]*

Endnotes for Historian B
[Continued from previous page.]

[2] John Trenchard and Thomas Gordon, two writers of the English Civil War period, were particularly popular in America. These writers warned that standing armies and corruption were a threat to liberty. [See Elizabeth Cook, *Literary Influences in Colonial Newspapers, 1704–1750* (New York, 1912).]

For information on the Quakers merchants' interest in these writers, see Frederick Tolles, *Meeting House and Counting House* (Chapel Hill, NC: 1948), pp. 178–9.

Evidence that American pamphleteers used the ideas of these writers is indexed in Bernard Bailyn, *Pamphlets of the American Revolution,* vol. 1 (Cambridge, MA: 1965).

[3] "Cato's Letters," a series of letters referring to Rome which appeared in the *London Journal* and later in book form, were particularly popular in the colonies and were used by American pamphleteers, such as Daniel Dulany, Sr., in their arguments.

[4] John Dickinson wrote in "Letters from a Farmer in Pennsylvania...," the most influential pamphlet published in America before 1776, that the Stamp Act, because it was small, might trap the colonists into accepting it, leading to a decline in liberty. (Philadelphia, 1768: John Harvard Library, Pamphlet 23).

[5] Benjamin Franklin said the customs officials generally "come only to make money as fast as they can." [*Writings of Benjamin Franklin,* ed. Albert H. Smyth, (New York, 1905–1907), V, 83.]

William Drayton stated that if judges were "men who depended upon the smiles of the crown for their daily bread," the possibility of an independent judiciary as an effective check on the executive (King, Prime Minister) would be lost. ["A Letter from a Freeman of South Carolina" (Charleston, 1774: John Harvard Library, Pamphlet 45), pp.10, 20.]

[6] Andrew Eliot wrote to a fellow colonist on June 28, 1770, that the Boston Massacre "serves to show the impossibility of our living in peace with a standing army."

Also, from testimony at the Boston Town Meeting, "Our houses, and even our bed chambers, are exposed to be ransacked" due to the writs of assistance. [*Votes and Proceedings of Boston* (1770, John Harvard Library).]

The American Revolution: Historian C (1940)

(1) A number of factors, including the French and Indian War and disputes over political liberty, led to the American Revolution. These causes themselves, however, were actually a result of a more fundamental underlying cause—economics. The basic conflict between England and her colonies was over British policies (laws, actions) which consistently helped British capitalists (businessmen) at the expense of the colonial economy.

(2) The British Empire of the late 1700s operated on an economic theory called *mercantilism*. The idea of mercantilism was to make the mother country, England in this case, prosperous. To accomplish this, British capitalists had to be protected and ensured of adequate profits. This all seemed reasonable to the British, but in the process, colonial manufacturing was prohibited; colonial currency was manipulated; colonial trade was regulated; colonial expansion was prevented; and colonial markets were threatened by British monopolies.

(3) British laws were designed to prevent the colonies from competing with products manufactured in England. To this end, the colonists were not allowed to manufacture certain products, such as iron (Iron Act), and were allowed to sell certain products they did manufacture, such as hats (Hat Act) and some textiles (Woolen Act), only to England. Other laws, meanwhile, encouraged the colonies to export raw materials—such

[Continued on next page.]

Historian C (1940)
[Continued from previous page.]

as cotton, copper, and furs—to England, where British companies manufactured them into finished products and sold them back to the colonists at higher prices and a handsome profit.

(4) British laws also controlled colonial currency. As a result of trade restrictions, hard currency (coins, gold, and silver) flowed in only one direction—out of the colonies and into England. Due to the shortage of hard currency, the colonists were forced to print paper money, which did not hold its value the way coins did. Colonists wanted to pay British companies in paper money, but the Currency Act, passed by Parliament in 1764, outlawed the use of paper money. In 1765, Colonist John Dickinson described the effect of this act on the colonies, saying, "Trade is decaying and all credit is expiring. Money is becoming so extremely scarce that reputable freeholders find it impossible to pay their debts… "

(5) With no large-scale manufacturing to attract their investment money, capitalists in the northern colonies turned to trade. Although northern merchants traded with many countries, here again, trade was restricted to benefit British capitalists. Colonists were prohibited (forbidden) from trading certain enumerated (listed) products directly with other countries; such products had to be shipped through England first, then to other countries or to the colonies.

(6) The largest colonial trade was with the West Indies (islands in the Caribbean). Sugar was brought in from the West Indies, made into rum (there were 63 rum distilleries in 1750 in Massachusetts alone), then sold or traded for products in many countries, most notably for slaves in Africa. The slaves, in turn, were taken to the West Indies and traded for more sugar. The sugar plantations on the British islands in the West Indies (for example, Jamaica and Barbados) were, however, so poorly run that the sugar there was more expensive than on the Spanish, French, Dutch, or Danish islands. Naturally, the colonists bought most of their sugar from these other islands.

(7) British sugar plantation owners pushed Parliament for laws to force the colonists to buy sugar only from the British islands. This monopoly situation would allow the plantations to sell all their sugar at a higher price. The owners had powerful friends in Parliament and were joined in their request by merchants and manufacturers who depended on the profits of sugar plantations for their own businesses. Moreover, British capitalists had spent a staggering £30 million developing the islands' plantations. This amount was six times as great as all British investments in continental North America. Is it any wonder that Parliament favored the West Indies plantation owners over the colonial merchants? The Molasses Act (1733) and the Sugar Act (1764) forced colonies to pay high taxes on sugar traded with islands other than the British West Indies.

(8) Still another area of colonial economic activity was investment in land. As the soil became depleted (drained of nutrients necessary for growing crops) in the East, colonial investors naturally looked for land further west. Here again, however, the colonists ran into British capitalists,

[Continued on next page.]

Historian C (1940)

[Continued from previous page.]

for the powerful Hudson Bay Company traded furs with the Indians. If colonists settled the land, it would end this profitable fur trade. The result was predictable. Parliament passed the Proclamation of 1763, which prohibited (forbade) colonists from settling beyond the Appalachian Mountains. The Quebec Act of 1774 went even further in restricting colonial economic activity in western areas.

(9) With the stiffened competition between colonial and British capitalists in the 1760s and 1770s, the British government began stricter enforcement of trade laws. Customs Commissioners were appointed to catch smugglers. Writs of assistance allowed officials to search for smuggled goods, and vice-admiralty and admiralty courts were set up to make sure smugglers were punished. Every possible weapon was to be used to weaken the smugglers, a group so threatening to British capitalists because it would not submit to British economic controls.

(10) In 1773 Parliament passed the Tea Act. This law allowed the British East India Company to sell its excess tea (17 million pounds) directly to Americans without taxes or restrictions. Once again, an act of Parliament helped a British company at the expense of the colonies, for the Act bypassed all Americans who shipped, imported, or sold British tea— or even Dutch tea, which was now more expensive. The British East India Company would soon have a monopoly of the American tea market. A Philadelphia pamphleteer, who called himself "A Mechanic," warned, "They will send their own factors and creatures, establish houses among us, ship us all other East India goods,...and undersell our merchants, 'till they monopolize the whole trade."

(11) The result of these many British economic restrictions was the American Revolution. Colonial capitalists—whether landowners, investors, fur dealers, or merchants— were converted from contented and loyal subjects into rebellious enemies of the crown. Their discontent transferred into the other classes, for the prosperity of the lower class was tied to the prosperity of the rich capitalists. Restrictive British legislation after 1763 led to an economic depression. Bankruptcy confronted merchants and large landowners; seamen and laborers were thrown out of work; small tradesmen and farmers faced financial ruin.

(12) Those who believe that the main cause of the American Revolution was the British debt from the French and Indian War should ask themselves, "Why weren't more acts passed to raise revenue?" "Why were the Stamp Act and Townshend Act so quickly repealed?" "Why, even after 1763, were most acts designed to control colonial economic activity?"

(13) Likewise, those who believe that political rights were the key to the Revolution should ask, "Why was most of the conflict over economics, for example, the Sugar Act, the customs officials, and the Tea Act?" The struggle between America and Great Britain was not over high-sounding political concepts, like taxation or natural rights. It was over colonial manufacturing, wild lands and furs, sugar, tea, and currency. Economic conflict was the key to the American Revolution.

LESSON 16   Was the Stamp Act Justified or Were the Colonists Justified in Not Paying It?

Each excerpt in this lesson is quoted from the source listed above it, even though none appear in quotation marks. Where quotation marks are used within an excerpt, the enclosed words were quoted in the given source from somewhere else. Spelling, punctuation, and capitalization have been modernized, and indicated sources have been summarized or rephrased for clarity.

1   D. Duane Cummins [historian], *The American Revolution* (Beverly Hills, CA: Benzinger, 1973), p. 27.

> Stamp duties as a source of revenue had been used with success in England for some time. The colonies of Massachusetts and New York had passed stamp duties of their own during the 1750s.

2   George Grenville [in quotation marks]; quoted in Edmund S. and Helen M. Morgan [historians], *The Stamp Act Crisis: Prologue to Revolution* (New York: Macmillan, 1963), p. 77.

> Grenville announced a [one-year] delay...in the Stamp Act. The reason,... he explained, was "that the colonies might take advantage of the delay to offer any objections they might have to the tax, or to suggest some more satisfactory tax, or to raise the money themselves in any way they saw fit."

3   Charles Garth [Colonial spokesman in London] to Committee of Correspondence, South Carolina Assembly, June 5, 1764; reprinted in *English Historical Review*, 54 (1939), 646–8. [Letter summarized and rephrased for this text.]

> Since I wrote you last, the Colonial Agents (spokesmen for the colonies) had a meeting with Mr. Grenville. [This meeting took place a short time after the announcement of the one-year delay of the Stamp Act.] We asked Mr. Grenville for copies of the proposed Stamp Act so we could take it back to the people in the colonies. Then the colonists would be far better able to decide whether or how far to approve or disapprove of it. But Mr. Grenville told us he couldn't show us a copy of the Stamp Act for two reasons. First, the Stamp Bill (Act) had not been put in its final or best form. Second, he felt the colonists shouldn't have any objections to it anyway because it seemed only natural for the colonists to pay their fair share of taxes for the defense of America. [England] was in immense debt, he said, and needed all the assistance it could get from the colonies.
>
> Mr. Grenville then said that he had made the one-year delay out of his good will for the colonists in America. He had thought a great deal about the tax and felt it was the best for the colonies. The colonies would have had great difficulties coming up with a tax, anyway. So when the colonists considered

[Continued on next page.]

[Continued from previous page.]

the Stamp Act he said they would agree it was the best for America, and he would be glad to take it to Parliament with the colonists' approval.

He said that some colonies might object that they couldn't afford the tax, but that those objections would carry little weight with Parliament. He mentioned that the stamp tax [collected by the Post Office] in New York showed that Parliament had the right to put on a stamp tax. We asked him about the items to be taxed and the amount of the tax and he said he would consult with us before meeting with Parliament to receive our ideas on those points.

4   Cummins, *American Revolution,* p. 62.

After proposing the stamp tax, George Grenville allowed a one-year delay prior to its enforcement. This apparent concession, in reality, gave the colonies a year to *agree* to the stamp tax. Grenville knew the colonies would not suggest alternative measures themselves.

5   Jack M. Sosin [historian], *Agents and Merchants* (Lincoln, NE: University of Nebraska Press, 1965), p. 54.

In no case did the provincial [colonial] legislatures in North America propose a practical alternative to the stamp bill or allow their agents [in London] grounds for compromise.

6   John Ploughshare [Englishman], "I Am for Old England," *London Chronicle*, 20 February 1766.

When the peace came [in the French and Indian War in 1763] and I understood that...[the British Empire] had got all America to ourselves, I thought it would be a great thing for old England, and that our fellow-subjects in that part of the world would trade with us more extensively than ever and be ready to contribute, according to their abilities, to the payment of our debts and taxes, especially as a great part of the debt...[was caused by] the late [French and Indian] war, undertaken...[for the benefit of the colonies], and ending to their advantage. When I heard that they were mobbing the King's Officers and declaring openly that the Parliament of England had no right to tax them, I was as much astonished as if a field where I had sowed barley should turn up peas... .

I think it no shame to say that I am for Old England; and I hold it neither fair nor honest in the Americans and their advocates to say that they will not pay any part of the expense even of that army which defends them against the savages.

[Continued on next page.]

[Continued from previous page.]

7   William Pym [Englishman], "The British Parliament Can at Any Time Set Aside All the Charters," [London] *General Evening Post*, 20 August 1765.

> The people of the colonies know very well that the taxes of the Mother Country (England) are every day increasing; and can they expect that no addition whatsoever will be made to theirs? They know very well that a great part of our national debt was contracted in (because of) establishing them on a firm foundation, and protecting them from the arbitrary attempts of their implacable enemies [the Indians and the French]. To be sure, Sir, in assisting the colonies we had an eye to our own interest. It would be ridiculous otherwise to squander away our blood and our treasure in their defense. But certainly the benefit was mutual; and consequently the disadvantage should be mutual, too.

8   Anti-Sejanus [pseudonym; Englishman], "The Whole Stamp Act Appears to Be Unexceptionable," *London Chronicle*, 28–30 November 1765.

> [The stamp tax] does not oppress the manufacturer, does not impede trade, does not fall upon any of the common necessaries of life, nor affect the poorer class of people…. It is levied (put) upon men of property and opulence (great wealth); and is so small a tax that it will hardly be felt.

9   Statement in Parliament at the passage of the Stamp Act, March 1765, quoted in Bernhard Knollenberg [historian], *The Origins of the American Revolution* (New York: Macmillan, 1960), p. 206.

> And now will these Americans, children planted by our care, nourished up by our indulgence (lenience) until they are grown to a degree of strength and opulence (wealth), and protected by our arms, …[complain about giving] their mite [money] to relieve us from the heavy weight of that burden which we lie under (debt from the French and Indian War)?

10 Colonel Isaac Barre [Member of Parliament], argument in Parliament, quoted in Knollenberg, *Origins of Revolution*, pp. 206–7.

> They (colonists) planted by your (English) care? No! Your oppressions planted them in America. They fled from your tyranny to a then-uncultivated and unhospitable country—where they exposed themselves to almost all the hardships to which human nature is liable….
>
> They nourished up by *your* indulgence (lenience)? They grew by your neglect of them. As soon as you began to care about them, that care was exercised in sending persons to rule over them….
>
> They protected by *your* Arms? They have nobly (heroically) taken up arms in your (England's) defense….

[Continued on next page.]

[Continued from previous page.]

11 Resolutions of the Stamp Act Congress, New York, October 19, 1765. A summary of each section appears in brackets [ ].

The members of this Congress...esteem it our indispensable duty to make the following declarations of our humble opinion [regarding] several late Acts of Parliament (the Stamp Act):

I   That his Majesty's subjects in these colonies, owe the same allegiance to the Crown of Great Britain, that is owing from his subjects born within the realm, and all due subordination to that august body the Parliament of Great Britain. [Americans owe the same loyalty to the King and Parliament as do the people of England.]

II   That His Majesty's...subjects in these colonies, are entitled to all the ...rights and liberties of his natural born subjects within the kingdom of Great Britain. [Americans have the same rights as Englishmen.]

III   That it is inseparably essential to the freedom of a people, and the undoubted right of Englishmen, that no taxes be imposed on them, but with their own consent, given personally, or by their representatives. [No taxation without representation.]

IV   That the people of these colonies are not, and from their local circumstances cannot be, represented in the House of Commons in Great Britain. [Americans cannot be represented in Parliament.]

V   That the only representatives of the people of these colonies are persons chosen therein by themselves, and that no taxes ever have been, or can be constitutionally imposed on them, but by their respective legislatures. [Only American legislatures can tax Americans.]

VI   That all supplies to the Crown, being free gifts of the people, it is unreasonable and inconsistent with the principles and spirit of the British Constitution, for the people of Great Britain to grant to His Majesty the property of the colonies. [The Stamp Act is unconstitutional.]

VII That trial by jury is the inherent and invaluable right of every British subject in these colonies. [Americans have the right of trial by jury.]

VIII That the late Act of Parliament, entitled "An Act for Granting Certain Stamp Duties, and Other Duties in the British Colonies and Plantations in America, etc." [the Stamp Act], by imposing taxes on the inhabitants of these colonies, and the said Act, and several other Acts, by extending the jurisdiction of the courts of Admiralty beyond its ancient limits, have a manifest tendency to subvert the rights and liberties of the colonists. [The Stamp Act wrongly extends the jurisdiction of Admiralty Courts, where there is no trial by jury.]

IX   That the duties imposed by several late Acts of Parliament, from the peculiar circumstances of these colonies, will be extremely burdensome and grievous; and from the scarcity of specie (gold and silver) the payment of them absolutely impracticable. [Americans cannot pay the Stamp Act in the required gold or silver coins.]

[Continued on next page.]

[Continued from previous page.]

12 Cummins, *American Revolution*, p. 63.

> Virginia interpreted the [Stamp] tax as a means whereby members of Parliament could shift the tax burden from their constituents (the people in England whom they represented and who could vote them out of office) to the American colonists who had no representation in Parliament.

13 Ibid, p. 66.

> To many colonists the stamp tax represented but the first of many future taxes to be levied (put) against them in order to pay British extravagances (unnecessary spending). Americans were made aware of the vast amounts of money paid out in the form of pensions to British Officials, many of whom thought little of purchasing a coach for 800 Pounds or spending 10,000 Pounds on a lavish [party]. Colonists reasoned that the source of revenue (money) to support these expenditures (spending) and costs of future British wars was to be a tax upon themselves.

14 Ibid, p. 29.

> The act was expected to raise approximately 60,000 Pounds annually; this sum was to be used to purchase supplies for the troops stationed in America. Such a moderate [amount] did not impose any real hardships upon the colonists. The historian John C. Miller calculated that 60,000 Pounds "amounted to only one shilling per head (per person) in the colonies, or about one-third the value of a day's labor each year."

15 Soame Jenyns [Englishman, Member of Parliament], "The Objections to the Taxation—Considered," Pamphlet, 1765.

> If the towns of Manchester and Birmingham [England], sending no [actual] representative to Parliament, are notwithstanding there represented [by virtual representation], why are not the cities of Albany and Boston [America] equally represented in that assembly? Are they not alike British subjects? Are they not Englishmen? Or are they only Englishmen when they solicit for protection, but not Englishmen when taxes are required to enable this country to protect them?

16 George Grenville, written argument in *The Regulations Lately Made*, by Thomas Whately [Secretary to Grenville], 1765; quoted in Morgan, *Stamp Act*, pp. 105–6. [Summarized and rephrased for this text; see source 2 for citation].

> ...They (colonists) claim...the Privilege, ...common to all British Subjects, of being taxed only with their own consent, given by their Representatives....
>
> For the fact is that the inhabitants of the Colonies are represented in Parliament: they do not indeed [choose] the Members of that Assembly;
>
> *[Continued on next page.]*

[Continued from previous page.]

neither are nine-tenths of the people of *Britain* electors. The colonies are in exactly the same situation: All *British* subjects are really in the same [situation]; none are actually, all are virtually represented in Parliament, for every Member of Parliament sits in the House not as a Representative of his own Constituents [people in his district], but as one of that august (dignified) Assembly (Parliament) by which all the common [people] of *Great Britain* are represented. Their rights and their interests, however his own [District] may be affected by [the laws], ought to be the great objects of his attention, and the only rules for his conduct. [Translation: Members of Parliament should and do represent the good of all the people of England even when the good of all goes against the good of the people within their own districts. Thus, all citizens of the British Empire are virtually represented in Parliament.]

17 Morgan, *Stamp Act*, p. 109.

...[Sir Thomas Youge, Member of Parliament] pointed out that a Member of Parliament, after his election, is "the attorney of the people of England, and as such is at full freedom to act as he thinks best for the people of England in general. He may receive, he may ask, he may even follow the advice of his particular constituents (people in his District); but he is not obliged, nor ought he to follow their advice, if he thinks it inconsistent with the general interest of his country." By 1765, this was the general belief in England.

18 Daniel Dulaney [colonist], *The Claim of the Colonies*, pamphlet summarized in Morgan, *Stamp Act*, pp. 109–11.

In a preface to his pamphlet, Dulany acknowledged that "It would now be an unfashionable doctrine, whatever the ancient opinion might be, to affirm that the constituent can bind his representative by instructions." The reason why instructions by voters were not generally considered binding on representatives in England was that, as Grenville said, each member was considered the representative of those who did not participate in choosing him as well as of those who did. But this idea, despite its currency (popularity) had never been defined or carefully [examined]. Dulany, accepting it as far as England was concerned, attempted to determine the meaning, and the only way in which he could make sense of it was to assume that a dual representation was involved, whereby those who could participate in elections represented those who could not. In this way the members of Parliament actually represented the voters and virtually represented the non-voters. When this supposition was applied merely to England, it could be defended with some pretense of reason: it could be argued, for example, that voteless Leeds and Birmingham were adequately represented in a Parliament containing members from other industrial borroughs (towns) with similar

[Continued on next page.]

[Continued from previous page.]

interests. To extend the concept to the whole empire, however, was to reduce it to absurdity; to say that the voters of England had similar interests to the colonists was so far from true that in the matter of taxation the very reverse was true. [Dudley] admitted that it would be advantageous to both the Parliament and the people of Great Britain to load America with taxes, for every shilling that came to the Treasury from the colonies meant one shilling less to be collected at home. A tax raised in England would affect the legislators who voted for it and the electors who chose them as well as the non-voting population, but a tax raised by Parliament in America would affect the people who levied it only by reducing their total tax bill. In this situation to say that the Americans were virtually represented in Parliament was ridiculous.

It was not true, moreover, that there was a great deal of English land not represented in Parliament. Grenville, in maintaining this proposition, had been thinking only of the borough representation. It was well known that this was based on a distribution of population which had long since changed, leaving empty shells of towns with representatives while newly risen industrial centers had none. But in addition to borough representatives Parliament contained two members from each county, so that every square foot of English land was represented, if not by a special borough member, then at least by the two county members. No English property-holder, therefore, was in the same situation as an American, who could not participate in the election of any member. Not one acre of American ground was represented in Parliament; not one acre of English ground was unrepresented.

Even the most ardent advocates of virtual representation, as the conception had been defended before Grenville's time, had admitted the propriety of a member's hearing and possibly heeding the advice of his constituents and the right of his constituents to replace him at the next election if he did not. But to what member of Parliament could the Americans give advice? What member could they replace at the next election for violating their wishes? Instead of giving instructions they must appear as petitioners, humbly begging for favors. How could it be said, then, that Americans were represented in Parliament in anything like the way that Englishmen were?

LESSON 17   Who Fired First at Lexington Green?

Background Information

On April 19, 1775, a group of British soldiers marched into Lexington on their way to seize some colonial military supplies stored in Concord. They were met on Lexington Green by colonial militia led by Captain John Parker. In the next few moments shooting started and several colonists were killed. One question that has arisen about this event is "Who fired first?"

Why do you think it is important in a war to know who fired the first shot? Look at the map below and the evidence on the following pages. Write the strengths and weaknesses of each piece of evidence on the worksheet, then make up your mind who you think fired first. Spelling, capitalization, and punctuation were modernized throughout the evidence presented.

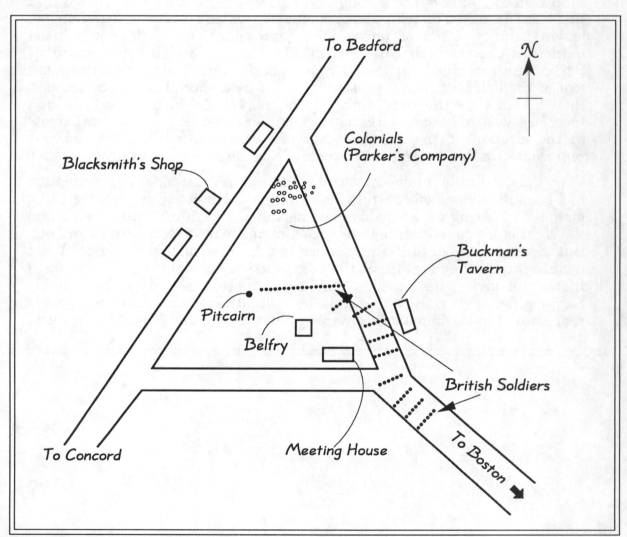

Figure 6: Map of Lexington Green, April 19, 1775.

[Continued on next page.]

1 Official deposition (testimony written down under oath) of John Parker, commander of the colonial militia.

> I, John Parker, of lawful age, and commander of the Militia in Lexington, do testify and declare, that on the nineteenth instant [April 19], [about one o'clock] in the morning..., being informed that there were a number of Regular (British) officers riding up and down the road, stopping and insulting people as they passed..., and also...that a number of regular troops were on the march from Boston in order to take the Province Stores at Concord, ordered our Militia to meet on the [Lexington] Common...to consult what to do. [We] concluded not to be discovered, nor meddle or make with said Regular Troops, if they should approach, unless they should insult us. Upon their sudden approach, I immediately ordered our Militia to disperse and not to fire. Immediately said Troops made their appearance, ...rushed furiously, fired upon and killed eight of our party without receiving any provocation therefore from us.

2 Personal diary of Lieutenant John Barker, a British officer.

> 19th. At 5 o'clock we arrived there and saw a number of people, I believe between two- and three-hundred, formed in a Common in the middle of the town; we still continued advancing, keeping prepared against an attack although without intending to attack them, but on our coming near them they fired one or two shots, upon which our men without any orders, rushed in upon them, fired and put them to flight; several of them were killed, we could not tell how many, because they got behind walls and into the woods. We had a man of the 10th Light Infantry wounded, nobody else hurt.

3 Sworn testimony of Thomas Fessenden, a colonial onlooker, to the Justices of the Peace in Middlesex County.

> *Lexington, April 23, 1775.* I, Thomas Fessenden..., testify and declare, that being in a pasture near the meeting-house at said Lexington on [last] Wednesday at about a half-hour before sunrise,...I saw three officers on horseback advance to the front of said Regulars, when one of them, being within six rods of the said Militia, cried out, "Disperse, you rebels, immediately," [and] brandished his sword over his head three times. Meanwhile the second officer, ...about two rods behind him, fired a pistol pointed at said Militia, and the Regulars kept huzzaing (yelling) until he had finished brandishing his sword, and when he had thus finished..., he pointed it down towards said Militia, and immediately...the said Regulars fired a volley at the Militia and then I ran off, as fast as I could, while they continued firing until I got out of their reach. I further testify that as soon as the officer cried "Disperse, you rebels," the said Company of Militia dispersed every way as fast as they could, and while they were dispersing the Regulars kept firing at them incessantly, and further saith not.
>
> *Thomas Fessenden*

[Continued on next page.]

[Continued from previous page.]

4   Official report of Major Pitcairn, commander of the advanced British party that first entered Lexington Green, to General Gage, his commander in Boston.

I gave directions to the troops to move forward, but on no account to fire, or even attempt it without orders. When I arrived at the end of the Village, I observed drawn up on a green near 200 of the Rebels. When I came within about one hundred yards of them, they began to file off towards some stone walls on our right flank. The Light Infantry, observing this, ran after them. I instantly called to the soldiers not to fire, but to surround and disarm them, and after several repetitions of those positive orders to the men—not to fire etc.—some of the Rebels, who had jumped over the wall, fired four or five shots at the soldiers, which wounded a man of the Tenth, and my horse was wounded in two places, from some quarter or other. At the same time several shots were fired from a Meeting House on our left. Upon this, without any order or regularity, the Light Infantry began a scattered fire, and continued in that situation for some little time, contrary to the repeated orders both of me and the officers that were present. It will be needless to mention what happened after, as I suppose Col. Smith has given a particular account of it, I am sir

Your most obedient humble Servant,

/s/ John Pitcairn
Boston Camp, 26th April, 1775

5   Sworn deposition of thirty-four colonial militiamen, submitted to the Justices of the Peace in Middlesex County.

Lexington, April 25, 1775   We, Nathaniel Mullekin, Philip Russell, Moses Harrington, Junior, Thomas and Daniel Harrington, William Grimer, William Tidd, Isaac Hastings, Jones Stone, Jr., James Wyman, Thaddeus Harrington, John Chandler, Joshua Reed, Jr., Joseph Simonds, Phineas Smith, John Chandler, Jun., Reuben Lock, Joel Viles, Nathan Reed, Samuel Tidd, Benjamin Lock, Thomas Winship, Simeon Snow, John Smith, Moses Harrington the third, Joshua Reed, Ebenezer Parker, John Harrington, Enoch Willington, John Hosmer, Isaac Green, Phineas Sterns, Isaac Durant, and Thomas Headly, Jr., all of lawful age, and inhabitants of Lexington, in the County of Middlesex, and Colony of the Massachusetts-Bay, in New England, do testify and declare, that on the nineteenth of April instant, about one or two o'clock in the morning, being informed that several officers of the [British] Regulars had, the evening before, been riding up and down the road, and had detained and insulted the inhabitants passing the same, and also understanding that a body of Regulars were marching from Boston towards Concord with intent, as it was supposed, to take the stores (military supplies) belonging to the Colony in that town, we

[Continued on next page.]

[Continued from previous page.]

were alarmed; and having met at the place of our Company's parade, were dismissed by our captain, John Parker, for the present, with orders to be ready to attend at the beat of the drum. We further testify and declare, that about five o'clock in the morning, hearing our drum beat, we proceeded towards the parade, and soon found that a large body of (British) Troops were marching towards us. Some of our Company were coming up to the parade, and others had reached it; at which time the Company began to disperse. Whilst our backs were turned on the Troops we were fired on by them, and a number of our men were instantly killed and wounded. Not a gun was fired by any person in our Company on the Regulars, to our knowledge, before they fired on us, and they continued firing until we had all made our escape.

6 Samuel Steinberg (historian), *The United States: Story of a Free People* (Boston: Allyn and Bacon, 1963), p. 92.

In April 1775, General Gage, the military governor of Massachusetts, sent out a body of troops to take possession of military stores at Concord, a short distance from Boston. At Lexington, a handful of "embattled farmers," who had been tipped off by Paul Revere, barred the way. The "rebels" were ordered to disperse. They stood their ground. The English fired a volley of shots that killed eight patriots. It was not long before the swift-riding Paul Revere spread the news of this new atrocity to the neighboring colonies. The patriots of all of New England, although still a handful, were now ready to fight the English. Even in faraway North Carolina, patriots organized to resist them.

7 Sworn testimony given by Sylvannus Wood (colonist) on June 17, 1826, to the Justices of the Peace.

The British troops approached us rapidly in platoons, with a General officer on horseback at their head. The officer came up to within about two rods of the center of the company, where I stood. The first platoon [was] about three rods distant (away). They there halted. The officer then swung his sword, and said, "Lay down your arms, you damn'd rebels, or you are all dead men—fire." Some guns were fired by the British at us from the first platoon, but no person was killed or hurt, being probably charged only with powder. Just at this time, Captain Parker ordered every man to take care of himself. The company immediately dispersed; and while the company was dispersing and leaping over the wall, the second platoon of the British fired, and killed some of our men. There was not a gun fired by any of Captain Parker's company within my knowledge.

[Continued on next page.]

[Continued from previous page.]

8 Sworn testimony given on April 23, 1775, by John Bateman, a British Regular captured by the colonists.

> I, John Bateman, belonging to the Fifty-second Regiment, commanded by Colonel Jones, on Wednesday morning on the nineteenth day of April instant, was in the party marching to Concord, being at Lexington in the County of Middlesex; being nigh (near) the meeting-house in said Lexington, there was a small party of men gathered together in that place when our Troopers marched by. I testify and declare that I heard the word of command given to the Troops to fire, and some of said Troops did fire. I saw one of said small party lay dead on the ground nigh said meeting-house, and I testify that I never heard any of the inhabitants so much as fire one gun on said Troops.

9 On June 10, 1775, a British newspaper, *The London Gazette*, printed this article about the Lexington affair.

> Lieutenant Nunn, of the Navy, arrived this morning at Lord Dartmouth's, and brought letters from General Gage, Lord Percy, and Lieutenant-Colonel Smith, containing the following particulars of what passed on the nineteenth of April last between a detachment of the King's Troops in the Province of Massachusetts-Bay and several parties of rebel Provincials... .
>
> Lieutenant-Colonel Smith, finding, after he had advanced some miles on his march, that the country had been alarmed by the firing of guns and ringing of bells, dispatched six Companies of Light-Infantry in order to secure two bridges on different roads beyond Concord. ...Upon their arrival at Lexington, [these troops] found a body of the country people, under arms, on a green close to the road; ...The King's Troops marching up to them, in order to inquire the reason of their being so assembled. They went off in great confusion, and several guns were fired upon the King's Troops, from behind a stone wall and also from the meeting house and other houses, by which one man was wounded, and Major Pitcairn's horse shot in two places. In consequence of this attack by the rebels, the troops returned the fire and killed several of them. After which the detachment marched on to Concord without anything further happening... .

Using a Chart to Evaluate Strengths and Weaknesses of Evidence

Q Using a chart like the one shown below, evaluate the evidence given in this lesson about who fired first at Lexington Green.

Evidence number	Author?	Who fired first?	Strengths of the evidence?	Weaknesses of the evidence?
1				
2				
3				
4				
5				
6				
7				
8				
9				

Q Based on this evidence, who fired first at Lexington Green? Give two reasons for your answer.

LESSON 18   Analyzing Pictures as Arguments

The following pages contain several pictures of the Battle of Lexington. Think of the pictures as arguments about how the battle went. Use the pictures, the diagram of Lexington Green on page 76, and the Relevant Information below to answer the questions.

Relevant Information

1. The Battle of Lexington took place around sunrise on April 19, 1775.
2. Evidence indicates that the British had few (maybe three or four) wounded (one of which was Major Pitcairns's horse) and none killed.
3. Muskets, which were used by both sides, were inaccurate weapons.
4. The colonists had eight men killed and ten wounded.

Analyzing Pictures

Q Look at the pictures of Lexington Green and fill in this chart. You will have to guess at some answers.

Picture number	Artist pro-Colonial or pro-British?	When painted?	Does it seem accurate?	List any inaccuracies
1				
2				
3				
4				
5				

 Which of the pictures seems to be most accurate? Why do you think so?

Pictures of the Battle of Lexington

1.

Lexington (MA) Historical Society

2.

Brown Brothers

3.

Brown Brothers

[Continued from previous page.]

4.

Brown Brothers

5.

The Connecticut Historical Society

LESSON 19   Effects of the American Revolution

 The American colonies declared their independence from England in 1776. Seven years later, in 1783, England agreed to end the war, thereby recognizing the United States as an independent nation. What effects do you think the American Revolution had?

1.   Brainstorm a list of effects.

2.   a.   Choose one of the effects you projected and write it here.

      b.   What would you **expect** to find if that effect actually occurred. (For example, if you predicted that John came home before you, you might expect to see the light on in his room).

      c.   What evidence can you find which counts for your projection?

      d.   What evidence can you find which counts against your projection?

3.   Historians think in terms of social, political, intellectual, religious, economic, personal, and technological categories. Think of these categories as you look back at your brainstorm list (part 1). Are there areas you missed? If so, add them here. Try to have one effect for each category.

4.   Look at the groups of people you implied were affected by the Revolution (your answers to 1 and 2). List the groups you thought about, then list those you did not think about. How might the Revolution have affected those groups?

LESSON 20   Evaluating a Constitution

A written constitution for a government is summarized below. Read it, then answer the questions that follow.

We, the undersigned delegates of the thirteen states, agree to this constitution.

- Each state retains sovereignty (independence) and keeps every power not given in this constitution to the national government.

- This is a league of friendship for the common defense and general welfare of the people.

- Each state gets one vote in Congress. Congress passes laws. Delegates from each state are appointed to serve for one year by the state legislature.

- No state shall enter into an alliance (agreement) with a foreign government or fight a war on its own.

- State legislatures will decide on and collect taxes for the national government.

- Congress alone has the right to declare war, to make peace, and to raise (create) an army and navy. When states have a disagreement, they can come to Congress, which will set up commissioners to hear and settle the dispute.

- Congress can set the value of coins and can issue and borrow money.

- Nine of the thirteen states must approve bills on important issues before they pass as laws.

- All debts owed by this government will be paid.

- Changes to this constitution must be approved by every state.

Q Based on the summary above, answer each of the following.

- What, if any, are the strengths of this constitution?

- What, if any, are the weaknesses of this constitution?

- What is your overall judgment of this constitution?

- What changes would you suggest to improve this constitution?

[Continued on next page.]

Analyzing the Governing Constitution, 1781–1787

1. List the powers given to the national government by this constitution.

2. Are these powers enough? What other powers should this constitution grant to the national government in order to make it effective? Think of political and economic powers.

3. What is a possible weakness, if any, in each of the following parts of the constitution? That is, what problems might arise from each of these?

   a. Every power not given to the national government by this constitution remains with the individual states.

   b. Every state gets one vote in Congress.

   c. Delegates are appointed by state legislatures for a one-year term.

   d. State legislatures will determine (decide on) and collect taxes.

   e. Nine states must approve any bill before it can become a law.

   f. Changes in the constitution must be approved by every state.

4. Sovereignty is defined as "supreme power; the right to decide for your group." A group with sovereignty cannot legitimately be told what to do by another group. Who (the national government or the states' governments) has sovereignty in this constitution? Explain your answer.

5. List at least three beliefs held by the writers of this constitution.

6. This constitution was approved to start the United States government in 1781. Based on what you have learned in your history course so far, how was this constitution an outgrowth of American experience before 1781?

[Continued on next page.]

Relevant Information: United States Government, 1781–1787

1. Many Americans owe money to Britain, and Britain wants to be paid.

2. Britain owns and occupies a number of forts between the Appalachian Mountains and the Mississippi River, which it does not want to give up. The area where the forts are located was given to the United States by Britain in 1783.

3. Spain will not cooperate with the United States, refusing to give up land claims or to allow Americans use of the Mississippi River for trade.

4. Spain and Britain are supplying Indians with guns and encouraging them to fight American pioneers.

5. The United States has a huge debt in terms of both principal and interest.

6. Different states have different money.

7. State legislatures are being pressured by people in their state to protect their businesses from competition in other states.

8. During the American Revolution the British did not sell products in America, which led to the growth of American businesses. After the war (1783) Britain again started to sell products in the United States, frequently for lower prices than American companies charged. As a result, some American businesses have gone bankrupt.

9. After the American Revolution the British closed the British West Indies to American trade. Many Americans have gotten around the law, however, and continue to trade with the West Indies.

10. Various states claimed Western areas, but some states have given up their claims.

Q Based on the information above and the summary on page 87, how effective do you think this government was in dealing with America's problems during the years 1781–1787? Explain your answer and support it with specific references.

LESSON 21   Shays's Rebellion

Read the following interpretations and write an evaluation of them. Ask yourself what each historian is arguing and how well each supports his or her claims.

Shays's Rebellion: Historian A

(1)   In the fall of 1786, a group of Massachusetts farmers, led by Daniel Shays and others, rose in rebellion. They demanded that no more farmers be jailed for failing to pay debts. In January 1787 Shays's men even attacked the federal arsenal in Springfield. Finally defeated by the state militia in February, the rebels had nevertheless thrown Massachusetts into a state of turmoil for months.

(2)   When delegates to the Constitutional Convention met in Philadelphia in the summer of 1787, they strengthened the central government. They had obviously learned a lesson from the recent Rebellion. They could see that the Articles of Confederation were too weak to prevent such uprisings. Daniel Shays and his rebels had contributed greatly to the writing of the Constitution.

Evaluation:

[Continued on next page.]

    © 1990 *MIDWEST PUBLICATIONS*, P.O. Box 448, Pacific Grove, CA 93950

[Continued from preceding page.]

Shays's Rebellion: Historian B

(1) Although the farmers involved in Shays's Rebellion were not interested in outright revolution, and although they were quickly crushed by the Massachusetts state militia, they spread alarm throughout the country in 1786 and 1787. Every state had its share of debt-ridden farmers who might take it into their heads to revolt.

(2) Many delegates to the Constitutional Convention of 1787 were men of property. They were unsettled by the threat to property symbolized by the rebellious actions of the Shaysites. They wrote a strong central government into the new Constitution to prevent such threats to property and to the Union.

(3) George Washington had hesitated even to attend the Constitutional Convention. After Shays's Rebellion he wrote, "No day ever dawned more favorably than ours did; and no day was ever more clouded than the present.... We are fast verging to anarchy and confusion!"[1] In March 1787 Washington, having been pushed out of retirement by the Rebellion in Massachusetts, decided to attend the Constitutional Convention.

Endnote for Historian B

[1] Washington to James Madison, *The Writings of George Washington, 1745–1799*, ed. John C. Fitzpatrick (Washington, D.C.: 1931–1944), XXIX, pp. 33–4.

Evaluation:

[Continued on next page.]

Evaluating Viewpoints on Shays's Rebellion

 Historian A is arguing about a cause of an important event (the effect).

1. a.   What is the cause?

   b.   What is the effect?

2.   When people make a cause-and-effect argument, they are supposed to show the connection between the cause and the effect. That is, they are supposed to show how and why the cause led to the effect.

   For example, suppose I said that you were angry with me (the effect) because I got an A on the last test (the cause). I should show some evidence that it's the test that made you angry—for example, a note you wrote to a friend saying that you hate me because I got an A. If I haven't any evidence to show the connection between the test score and your anger, then my argument isn't very strong. After all, maybe you don't even know what I got on the test, or maybe you're angry about something else.

   Look back at the cause and the effect you wrote for question 1. Does Historian A show how the cause led to the effect? Does he show the connection between the cause and the effect? Explain your answer.

3.   Overall, how strong is Historian A's argument?

 Historian B also presents a cause-and-effect argument.

4.   How well does Historian B show the connection between Shays's Rebellion (the cause) and the Constitution (the effect)?

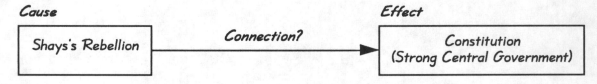

Cause   *Effect*

Shays's Rebellion   — *Connection?* →   Constitution (Strong Central Government)

5.   Overall, how strong is Historian B's argument? Explain your answer.

[Continued on next page.]

    © 1990 MIDWEST PUBLICATIONS, P.O. Box 448, Pacific Grove, CA 93950

Relevant Information: Shays's Rebellion

A. On at least five occasions before Shays's Rebellion, George Washington wrote that the Articles of Confederation were too weak and that the central government needed to be given more power. In 1779 he wrote, "We seem to be verging fast on destruction."

B. George Washington decided to attend the Constitutional Convention after Shays's Rebellion had been suppressed by the Massachusetts militia.

C. There were fifty-five delegates to the Constitutional Convention, which met for eighteen weeks.

D. In the spring of 1786, twelve of thirteen states had approved an amendment to the Articles of Confederation to give the central government revenue (money) from tariffs (taxes). All states had to ratify an amendment to the Articles, however, and New York voted against it. Many people now called for a convention to rewrite the Articles.

E. In September 1786 a convention met at Annapolis, Maryland, to consider uniform commerce for the states. It did not reform the commerce laws, but rather called for a convention to consider other changes in the Articles. The Annapolis Convention ended before news of Shays's Rebellion reached it.

F. Shays's Rebellion was mentioned by nine speakers at the Constitutional Convention. Four of those speakers did not sign the Constitution. (This indicates that they probably did not approve of it.)

G. Two of the delegates who mentioned Shays's Rebellion used it to argue against the Constitution. Eldrige Gerry said, "More blood would have been spilt in Massts in the late insurrection, if the Genl. authority (central government) had intermeddled." [Paul L. Ford, ed., *Pamphlets on the Constitution of the United States, Published During Its Discussion by the People 1787–1788* (Brooklyn: 1888), pp. 1–23.]

H. Leading supporters of the Constitution, called Federalists, were convinced of the need for a stronger government long before Shays's Rebellion. James Madison and Alexander Hamilton had frequently written of the need for more central power, mainly to regulate commerce and raise tax money.

I. Three of the four Massachusetts delegates did not sign the Constitution.

J. After the Constitution had been written, it had to be ratified. People who supported ratification were called Federalists; people who opposed ratification were called Antifederalists. Some of the people who opposed Shays's Rebellion were Federalists and some were Antifederalists. Likewise, some who supported the Rebellion were Federalists and some were Antifederalists.

K. The delegate from Massachusetts who did sign the Constitution, Rufus King, had been opposed to it until after Shays's Rebellion had been defeated in February 1787. In early February, people were talking about choosing King as a delegate if Massachusetts sent anyone.

[Continued on next page.]

[Continued from previous page.]

L. *The Anarchiad*, a series of poems, songs, and odes, was published in twelve issues and widely reprinted in Federalist newspapers. (Federalists were supporters of the Constitution). One such poem, referring to Shays's Rebellion, was

> See the jails open, and the thieves arise.
> Thy Constitution, Chaos, is restor'd;
> Law sinks before thy uncreating word;
> Thy hand unbars th' unfathomed gulf of fate,
> And deep in darkness 'whelms the new-born state.

M. The Congress under the Articles of Confederation voted on February 21, 1787, to ask the states to send delegates to Philadelphia for the Constitutional Convention.

N. In September 1786, before news of Shays's Rebellion had spread, five states sent delegates to the Annapolis Convention for the purpose of reforming the Articles of Confederation. In May 1787, after Shays's Rebellion, twelve of the thirteen states sent delegates to the Philadelphia Convention for the same purpose.

 Use the Relevant Information (above) to answer the following questions.

1. What does the information say about the connection between Shays's Rebellion and the Constitution?

2. Does the information suggest that there might be other, more important causes for the Constitution? If so, what are these possible causes?

3. Based on the information you have, do you think the Constitution would have been written—and written in basically the same form—without Shays's Rebellion? Explain your answer.

4. Was Shays's Rebellion an important cause of the Constitution? Explain your answer.

LESSON 22   Evaluating Sources

When someone makes a claim, that person should give information, as well as the source of the information, to support the claim. The source is usually the person, the written document, or the object from which the information came, although it may also be based on the personal observations or experiences of the person making the claim.

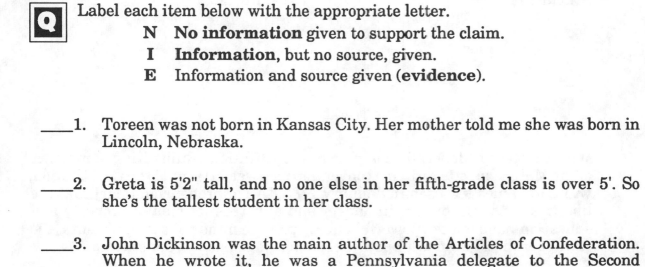

Q Label each item below with the appropriate letter.

    N **No information** given to support the claim.

    I **Information**, but no source, given.

    E Information and source given (**evidence**).

_____1. Toreen was not born in Kansas City. Her mother told me she was born in Lincoln, Nebraska.

_____2. Greta is 5'2" tall, and no one else in her fifth-grade class is over 5'. So she's the tallest student in her class.

_____3. John Dickinson was the main author of the Articles of Confederation. When he wrote it, he was a Pennsylvania delegate to the Second Continental Congress.

_____4. In a January 1776 letter, John Adams showed his optimism for the new government when he said. "[This is a] period when a coincidence of circumstances…has afforded to thirteen Colonies, at once, an opportunity of beginning government anew from the foundation, and building as they choose. How few of the human race have ever had any opportunity of choosing a system of government for themselves and their children!"

_____5. The Northwest Ordinance of 1787 was probably the Confederation Congress's most important piece of legislation.

_____6. The fifty-five men who made up the Constitutional Convention were a remarkable group. For example, in an age when few Americans went to college, a majority of the delegates were college graduates.

_____7. Some delegates to the Constitutional Convention argued that the convention must follow their instructions to amend the Articles of Confederation. Alexander Hamilton argued they should write a new constitution. The convention sided with Hamilton when it agreed to Edmund Randolph's resolution to establish a national government.

[Continued on next page.]

[Continued from previous page.]

 Evaluate the following pieces of evidence by listing strengths and weaknesses of each. Remember, you are deciding how strong each is as a source of information. The key question is "Can we believe what the source says?" For help on the criteria for evaluating evidence, see the section on **Evidence** in the "Guide to Critical Thinking" (Unit 1).

8. Why do many of the students in Bob's class dislike him? Bob told Peter that the other kids in his class don't like him because he's so much better than anyone else at all sports.

   STRENGTHS: WEAKNESSES:

9. Why did the Antifederalists oppose the constitution? Rufus King, a member of the Massachusetts ratifying convention who was in favor of the Constitution, wrote to James Madison in January 1788, "An apprehension [fear] that the liberties of the people are in danger and a distrust of men of property and education have a more powerful effect upon the minds of our opponents [the Antifederalists] than any specific objections against the Constitution."

   STRENGTHS: WEAKNESSES:

10. Why were supporters of the Constitution successful in getting it ratified? In their book *The United States,* historians Winthrop Jordan, Leon Litwack, Richard Hofstadter, William Miller, and Daniel Aaron state that several factors were important to getting the Constitution ratified, among which were "At the national level it is clear that leaders who favored the new Constitution had the edge in talent."

   STRENGTHS: WEAKNESSES:

LESSON 23   Arguments over Constitutional Ratification

Background Information

The original government of the United States, called the Articles of Confederation, was comprised of a weak central government and very strong state governments. The Constitution written in 1787 made the central government much stronger and the state governments weaker. In the struggle to get the new Constitution ratified (approved) supporters of the Constitution were called Federalists, while opponents were called Antifederalists.

This lesson contains two arguments on whether or not the Constitution should be approved. The first argument, "Federalist Paper 10," was written by James Madison as part of *The Federalist Papers*, a series of newspaper essays in favor of ratification in New York. The second argument, known as the "'Brutus' Essay," was also printed in New York newspapers and was probably written by the Antifederalist Robert Yates,

a New York judge. The name "Brutus" was used to convey the idea of the heroic Roman republican (the Antifederalists) who killed the tyrant Caesar (the new, tyrannical Constitution).

The two arguments focus on how to control factions in society and promote the public good. A *faction* is a group of people, such as farmers, with a common interest. For example, the owners of automobile companies may follow the interest of their faction by opposing pollution control devices on cars because it will increase manufacturing costs. On the other hand, these owners may decide against their own factional interests and support the antipollution devices for the good of the country at large; i.e., the public good.

These arguments focus on the question, "What kind of government is most likely to control self-interest and promote decisions based on the public good?"

Argument A

(1) People in all societies tend to organize into factions or groups to promote what is good for **them** rather than what is good for society in general. We should concern ourselves with how to deal with these factions and promote the public good, that is, the good of society in general.

(2) One option is to control the causes of factions. We could destroy the liberty on which factions depend— but that is worse than having factions. We could make everyone have the same opinions, thereby eliminating factions—but that is impossible. It

seems clear, then, that factions cannot be prevented by controlling their causes.

(3) A second option is to control the effects of factions. Minority factions are not a serious problem, for when a faction is a minority it cannot legitimately (legally) take control of the government. When a faction is a majority, however, it can legally pass laws to help its own interests at the expense of the public good and to the detriment of the rights of other citizens. This

[Continued on next page.]

Argument A
[Continued from previous page.]

control by a majority faction is a real danger in a pure democracy (a small nation in which the people vote directly on laws and policy), for the majority can easily get together to promote its interests on particular issues. For example, a business faction might pass laws for the government to build roads that would help businessmen at taxpayers' expense.

(4) A republic (a large nation in which the people elect representatives to decide on laws and policy), on the other hand, has more people and more factions. It is more difficult for a majority to organize a faction on a particular issue, and it is harder for a faction to operate in a united way. Furthermore, representatives in a republic are a chosen body of citizens whose wisdom may best discern (recognize) the true interest of their country—the public good.

(5) Demagoguery (gaining power by appealing to the prejudices and/or ignorance of the masses of the people) is one possible problem that may arise in electing representatives. A large republic, however, would overcome this problem. Since there are more people from which to choose representatives, and since there are more people to vote on each representative, there is less possibility of demagoguery. As a result, a large republic is more likely to elect enlightened (knowledgeable) representatives.

(6) This new constitution, now proposed for the United States, strengthens the central government, thereby establishing our country as a large republic. Through this new constitution, we will be able to control the problem of factions and to promote the public good by electing enlightened men as representatives.

Argument B

(1) Our country is in a critical period with regard to our government. We have been offered a new constitution to consider, and we should consider it carefully. The main question for consideration is whether these thirteen states should be reduced to one great republic or should continue as thirteen confederated republics.

(2) It is clear that the government proposed under the new constitution will effectively consolidate the United States into one republic. State governments will have little power, while the federal (central) government will dominate (control things). According to Article 6 of the new constitution, the laws of the United States government "shall be the supreme law of the land," clearly dominant over state laws. The federal government will have the power to tax and raise an army—both of which give it power over the states. Additionally, Article 1, Section 8 of the new constitution declares "that Congress shall have power to make all laws which shall be necessary and proper for carrying into execution the foregoing powers." This clause could be interpreted to justify passing almost any law. Thus, the federal government will continuously expand its power at the expense of the states.

[Continued on next page.]

Argument B

[Continued from previous page.]

(3)   Given, then, that the constitution replaces thirteen confederated states with one great republic, the questions to consider are "Will it work? Will it help us remain free and strong?" The answer, clearly, is that it will not.

(4)   A free republic cannot succeed over such a large area with so many inhabitants. Many illustrious authorities could be used to support the point but I will content myself with quoting only two. In *Spirit of Laws,* the Baron de Montesquieu says, "It is natural to a republic to have only a small territory, otherwise it cannot long subsist. In a large republic there are men of large fortunes, and consequently of less moderation.... In a large republic the public good is sacrificed to a thousand views.... In a small one, the interest of the public is easier perceived, better understood, and more within the reach of every citizen; abuses are of less extent, and of course are less protected." (Ch. XVI, Vol. 1, Book VIII) The Marquis Beccarari holds the same opinion.

(5)   Moreover, history furnishes no examples of a free republic of a size anything like the United States. The Greek and Roman republics began small. When they extended their territories by conquests (war) and became large, their governments changed from free republics to some of the most tyrannical (unfree) governments that ever existed.

(6)   If the people are to agree with the laws, representatives who pass the laws must know the people's views well enough to state the will of the people. If they do not know the people, then they can't speak for the people, and the people do not govern; power is in the hands of a few representatives. Since it is impossible for the representatives in a large republic to know the views of so many people, they can't pass laws in the name of the people. Increasing the number of representatives—so that each official represents a smaller number of people—doesn't work, because then there would be so many representatives that the government would be unwieldy (unable to function well).

(7)   In a large republic, such as the new constitution would provide, the people would know neither their representatives nor the reasons for their decisions. Suspicious of their representative's motives, people would not willingly support the laws. Thus, the government would have to use armed force to carry out the laws, and government by the people would be converted to government by force.

(8)   Thus, it can be seen that the proposed republic should be rejected. It will bring about a constant clash of views; it will cause strife which will slow governmental operation; and it will prevent decisions based on the public good.

Analyzing the Ratification Arguments

 Refer to Federalist Paper 10 [Argument A] to answer the following questions.

1. What is the main point of this argument?

2. Evaluate the cause-and-effect reasoning in the argument. What does the author say causes factions? How strong is the reasoning?

3. What other type(s) of reasoning (comparison, generalization, proof, eliminating alternatives) does this author use? Evaluate this reasoning. (Look in the "Guide to Critical Thinking" [Unit 1] if you need help.)

4. Based on this argument, list two of the author's (James Madison's) beliefs about good government.

5. Madison claims that a large republic will stop factions from dominating the government by preventing factions from getting together. Is this advantage also true today? (Think of the kind of reasoning you are using.)

 Refer to "Brutus' Essay I" [Argument B] to answer the following questions.

6. What is the main point of this argument?

[Continued on next page.]

[Continued from previous page.]

7.   What is the point of paragraph 2? How well does the author prove it?

8.   What type of reasoning (comparison, cause-and-effect, generalization, proof, eliminating alternatives) is used in paragraph 4? If you see more than one, write them all down. Evaluate one of the types of reasoning used.

9.   Identify and evaluate the reasoning used in paragraph 5.

10.   Evaluate the arguments presented in paragraphs 6 and 7.

11.   What assumptions does this author make? Watch especially for unstated assumptions.

Q Consider both arguments in answering the following.

12.   On what points, if any, do both authors agree?

13.   What is your view on how to achieve the public good? If you think the public good should not be emphasized, explain your position.

[Continued on next page.]

Making Government Policy: Factions vs. Public Good

 How do you think each group listed would answer the given question? Explain why you think so.

1. Should we have a tariff on foreign cars coming into the United States?
   a. American automobile companies

   b. American consumers

   c. United Auto Workers Union

   d. Car dealers

   e. Stockholders (investors) in American auto companies

2. Should the United States continue to operate nuclear power plants to generate electricity?
   a. Construction workers who build nuclear power plants

   b. Electric companies

   c. Consumers of electricity

   d. Coal companies (Note: Coal is also used to generate electricity.)

   e. Environmentalists

   f. People who live close to the power plants but don't work there

   g. Nuclear power plant workers

   h. Companies that supply nuclear power plants

   i. Stockholders in nuclear power plants

[Continued on next page.]

 © 1990 MIDWEST PUBLICATIONS, P.O. Box 448, Pacific Grove, CA 93950

[Continued from previous page.]

 Answer the following questions on government policy.

3. If you were a lawmaker—let's say a Senator—would it be better for the country in the long run for you to decide issues based on:
    — principles of right and wrong?
    — the interest of one group because that group has a great deal of political power or because you like that group?

Explain your answer.

4. Considering any issue—for example, the one on nuclear power plants in question 2—would it be better for the country in the long run to:
    — have one of the groups listed (i.e., the electric companies) control the government and pass laws to help its own interest?
    — have the various interests compete?
    — have the issue decided on its merits based on what is best for the country?

Explain your answer.

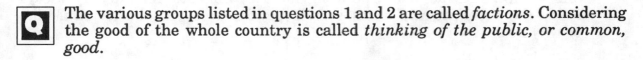 The various groups listed in questions 1 and 2 are called *factions*. Considering the good of the whole country is called *thinking of the public, or common, good*.

5. Do you think factions would ordinarily think of the public good in deciding an issue? Explain your answer.

6. How can a society get its people to consider the public good over their own self-interest?

[Continued on next page.]

[Continued from previous page.]

7. How can a government be set up to minimize the effects of factions and maximize consideration of the public good?

8. How can a government be set up to prevent a single faction or group of factions from taking control of the government?

9. Is it better for the country to have each representative chosen from a small or a large number of people? Explain your answer.

10. Should representatives always know how their constituents (citizens in their district) feel on issues before deciding how they will vote? Should they always follow their constituents' views, even if they disagree with those views? Why or why not?

LESSON 24   An Argument on the Constitution

The following summarizes arguments made by James Madison in three of the *Federalist Papers* favoring ratification (approval) of the Constitution. [For information on the issue of Constitutional ratification, see the **Background Information** for Lesson 23, page 101.] Read the argument, then evaluate it according to its reasoning and assumptions.

(1)   Our country is considering a change in government away from a confederation as established in the Articles of Confederation toward a more united government as proposed in the new Constitution. In our consideration, let us inquire about the history of confederations. Do they promote effective government? Do they protect liberty?

(2)   Four examples of confederacies shed light on these questions: the Amphyctionic Council and Achaean League of ancient Greece, and the Germanic Confederation and United Netherlands of more recent times. In each case the central government had powers of war and peace, the right to raise an army, and the ability to punish members—along with some economic and other powers. In each case the member cities or states were concerned about the danger of tyranny by the central government. In each case the real danger arose from the weakness of the confederation government.

(3)   The Amphyctionic Council failed because the more powerful cities, like Athens and Sparta, tried to dominate and corrupt the government. When the weaker cities sought outside help in their struggle with the stronger cities, Philip of Macedonia came to their aid and ended up conquering the whole confederation.

(4)   In the same way did Rome conquer the Achaean League, promising its members full independence from the League's rules and from any outside rule. The jealous members sided with Rome, and the divided league was easily conquered.

(5)   The Germanic Confederation and United Netherlands were weak because each member state felt it was sovereign, with the sole right to decide what it would do. Each state decided what was best for it and resisted the laws of the confederacy. Thus, the history of these confederacies is a history of wars, of bickering among members, of corruption of the strong and oppression of the weak, of insecurity against outside attack, and of member states failing to work for the general good of the confederacy.

(6)   Confederacies lasted as long as they did mainly because foreign governments wanted them to last. These foreign governments preferred known, weak confederacies to possibly strong, united governments.

(7)   These four examples show that confederations are weak and tend to fight among themselves. They may persevere (last) in ordinary times, but a serious crisis crumbles them and they fail. We must throw out our weak confederation government and replace it with the strong, united government proposed in the new constitution.

LESSON 25 Writing and Ratifying the Constitution: Two Interpretations of Motive

One of the great historical questions about the Constitution is why the delegates wrote it. In this lesson you will read two views of this subject. Read Historian A's viewpoint and evaluate it; *then* read Historian B's interpretation.

Historian A

(1) Suppose it could be shown that the Constitution was written and supported by one group of economic interests and that substantially all of the opposition came from a second economic group. Would it not be pretty conclusively demonstrated that the Constitution was not the product of an abstraction known as "the whole people" but of a group with economic interests who expected beneficial results from its adoption? This interpretation considers how economics influenced adoption of the Constitution.

(2) It should be noted at the outset that most people in the United States were not represented at all in the constitutional process. These powerless groups—slaves, indentured servants, women, and propertyless men—had no say in choosing delegates to the Constitutional Convention or to the ratifying conventions.

(3) Among the property-owning men, two broad groups struggled over adoption of the Constitution. The first group was composed of nonslave-owning landowners, mostly small farmers, almost all of whom were in debt for their land. They wanted more money to be issued, which, in turn, would increase prices for their farm products and give them more money with which to pay their loans. Before 1787 several state governments had tried such paper-money schemes to help farmers.

(4) The second group of property owners held personal property. This group included men who lent money at interest (creditors), slaveholders, land speculators, manufacturers, shippers, and owners of government securities. The strong national government proposed in the Constitution would ensure loan repayment, prevent slave revolts, and subsidize manufacturing and shipping through government improvements (such as improving harbors) and tariffs. Further, this group thought the Constitution would promote confidence in the government's ability to protect land from Indians and to pay off debts, resulting in increased land and government securities prices.

(5) Of the fifty-five men who wrote the Constitution, twenty-four lent money at interest, fifteen held slaves, fourteen were land speculators, eleven were involved in manufacturing and/or shipping, and forty held government securities.[1] The owners of government securities alone stood to gain $40 million by increasing the value of each security as much as twenty times.[2] This survey makes it obvious that the delegates to the Constitutional Convention had a definite economic stake in its writing.[3]

(6) As an economic document, the Constitution was designed to use its many checks on majority rule to protect property from the majority of people. The people do not directly elect either the president or, under the original Constitution, their senators. The

[Continued on next page.]

Historian A

[Continued from previous page.]

Supreme Court can prevent the popular majority from passing laws that would hurt property owners. In "Federalist Paper Number 10," James Madison argued that the government must prevent popular majorities from taking control of the government. He indicated that by "popular majority" he meant the propertyless and debtors when he stated, "Those who hold and those who are without property have ever formed distinct interests in society. Those who are creditors, and those who are debtors, fall under a like discrimination."[4]

(7)   The Constitution further protected property by preventing states from issuing paper money and from interfering with contracts. Thus, states could not help debtors get out of paying their loans.[5]

(8)   In addition to protecting property, the Constitution also provided positive powers—taxation, war, commercial control, and disposition of western lands—to help develop property. Through these powers, creditors would be paid in full, peace would be maintained, trading advantages with foreign nations would be gained, manufacturers would be protected, and western lands would be developed.

(9)   Enough has been outlined here to show that the idea of the Constitution as a piece of abstract legislation reflecting no economic interests is entirely false. It was an economic document written, with superb skill, by men whose property interests were immediately at stake.

(10) Supporters of the Constitution now had to persuade the states to ratify it. Analysis of the state ratifying conventions shows that, here again, support came mainly from coastal areas where manufacturers, creditors, and security holders were dominant, and the opponents mainly came from inland farm regions where debtors were dominant.[6] In several states where the majority of people were opposed to the Constitution, Constitutionalists used a number of tactics to overcome the opposition. In four states they scheduled the conventions early, before the opposition could get organized. And, since they were generally wealthier than the opposition, they could spend more money on their campaign to show the Constitution's advantages.

(11) In summary, most people had no say in the Constitution. The people who wrote and supported it were personally interested in and derived economic advantages from its ratification. The document they wrote was essentially economic and designed to protect private property, especially from popular majorities of the people. In five states, a majority of voters in elections for state conventions probably opposed ratification of the Constitution. Nevertheless, it was ratified because of the determination of leaders who also had an important economic interest in the Constitution. The Constitution was created, not by "the whole people," but rather by a consolidated economic group that knew what it wanted.

Endnotes for Historian A

[1] These statistics were taken from Treasury Department files and from biographies of the delegates.

[2] Many people who owned government securities in the 1780s doubted that the government under the Articles of Confederation would ever pay them back. Thus, they sold their securities cheaply, a $100 security selling for as little as $5–17. If the new government under the Constitution paid these securities off at full value, the new owners would receive $100, an amount up to twenty times more than the $5.00 they had paid to buy the security.

[Continued on next page.]

Endnotes for Historian A [Continued from previous page.]

[3] The purpose here is not, of course, to show that the Constitution was made for the personal benefit of the members of the convention. Rather, the important point is that they represented distinct groups whose economic interests they understood and protected.

[4] James Madison, "Federalist Paper, No. 10."

[5] For example, if a farmer owed a banker $2000 and couldn't pay it, under the new Constitution the state would be required to enforce the contract, making the farmer pay the loan in full or helping the banker take possession of the land.

[6] Orin Grant Libby, *Geographical Distribution of the Vote of the Thirteen States on the Ratification of the Federal Constitution, 1787-1788*, (Madison, WI: 1894).

Historian B

(1) Historian A wrote his economic interpretation of the Constitution in 1913. It has been a classic, towering over everything else written on the subject before or since. No other work on the making or nature of the Constitution has been so widely-debated, so widely-known, and, ultimately, so widely-accepted. This interpretation focuses on the question, "Is Historian A's thesis regarding the economic motives for the Constitution compatible with the facts?"

(2) Historian A claims that personal-property owners controlled the writing and ratification of the Constitution to benefit their own economic interests. The following information shows that this claim is not true.[1]

• Of the fifty-five delegates to the convention, thirteen had voted for such debtor relief as paper-money schemes; thirteen had economic interests that would be hurt by the Constitution; only nine made $1000 or more by the appreciation of securities under the Constitution. The major value in holdings of those at the convention was in farmland and slaves, not in personal property; thirty held government securities, but five of the top security holders voted against the Constitution.

• Since individual delegates had conflicting interests, it is difficult to group them as either real- or personal-property owners. For example, how would one categorize a debt-ridden merchant?

• Voting on the Constitution was by state (each state got one vote), not by individual, so it is impossible in most cases to tell how individual delegates voted. State votes on issues show no correlation to personal property interests versus real property interests.

• In those cases where delegates' personal votes can be figured out, they show no correlation to the delegate's economic interest. In fact, seven of the delegates who most opposed the Constitution were almost an all-star team of personal-property interests.

(3) The Constitution, contrary to Historian A's view, was not simply an economic document, although economic factors were certainly important. Most people in 1787 were property owners, so most were interested in the protection of private property. Property was not the only concern of those who wrote and ratified the Constitution, however, and we would do a grave injustice to the political philosophy and goals of the Founding Fathers if we assumed that property or personal gain was their only motive.

(4) Neither do the facts on ratification support Historian A's view. Only

[Continued on next page.]

Historian B

[Continued from previous page.]

in one or two states were opponents of the Constitution mainly farmers and supporters mainly personal-property owners from coastal areas. Indeed, we see a much more mixed picture. In some states, like Virginia, small farmers were for the Constitution; in other states, like Pennsylvania, holders of public securities were against the Constitution; in still other states, like Georgia, people voted for the Constitution so they would get a strong military to fight the Indians.[2] It is a much clearer distinction to say that those states which had done poorly under the Articles of Confederation government tended to favor the Constitution, and those which had done well tended to oppose it.

(5)   If the ratification conflict had been between large personal property interests on the one hand and small farmers and debtors on the other, there would have been no Constitution. Since an overwhelming percentage of the voters were small farmers, they could have rejected the new government with no trouble.

(6)   Historian A makes an issue of powerless groups who had no say in the Constitution. No slaves, indentured servants, or women could vote in any society at this time, so there was nothing unusual about their not voting on the Constitution. The issue of propertyless men has been exaggerated. Almost all adult men in the United States owned property, mostly as middle-class farmers. Thus, it is more likely that only five percent, rather than ninety-five percent, of the adult men were disenfranchised (not allowed to vote) due to property qualifications.

(7)   In summary, the Constitution was created about as much by the whole people as any government which embraced a large area and depended on representation (rather than direct participation) could be in the 1780s. The Constitution was written by men with a variety of motives, not just their own economic gain.

(8)   That the Constitution dealt with economic issues is normal and desirable. It protected property because most Americans owned property and wanted it protected—not from a large propertyless majority. The ratification struggle occurred over a wide variety of complex political, social, economic, geographic, and historical issues in each state—not over a simple conflict between small farmers and large personal property owners. Historian A's interpretation of the Constitution must be rejected as downright wrong in some areas and as highly simplistic and misleading in others.

Endnotes for Historian B

[1] Information on the fifty-five delegates is taken from biographies of the delegates, newspaper articles of the 1780s, and records of loans in the National Archives under the Register of Public Debt Certificates.

[2] Information on state ratification struggles is taken from records of state legislatures and ratification conventions (such as *Minutes of the Convention of the State of New Jersey, December 11, 1787,* and *Minutes of the General Assembly of the Commonwealth of Pennsylvania, 1781–1790*); from newspapers of the time (such as the *Virginia Herald*); from loan records in the National Archives; from banking and tax records in each state by county or town; from various geographic and population sources (such as Charles O. Paullin, *Atlas of the Historical Geography of the United States,* Washington, D.C., 1932, and Stella M. Sutherland, *Population Distribution in Colonial America,* New York, 1936), and various states' historical works.

LESSON 26   Foreign Views of the Constitution

The following viewpoints on the American Constitution are summaries of those presented in secondary school history textbooks of two foreign nations.

The Constitution of 1787 [Viewpoint A]

(1) A convention meeting in Philadelphia drafted the Constitution of 1787 which, with some amendments, still governs the United States of America.

(2) The convention named George Washington as President, and his prudent (cautious) action contributed to eliminating the violent opposition that appeared to impede (get in the way of) approval of a constitution.

(3) The Constitution of 1787 created a federal and democratic republic—organizing, on one hand, the central government with legislative, executive, and judicial powers, and on the other, relationships among the States of the American union.

(4) This Constitution, because of its democratic and republican nature and its structure, embodying (including) the division of powers for the first time, influenced Europe—through the French Revolution—and the rest of America through Latin American independence.

The Law Setting Up the Government [Viewpoint B]

The Constitution (from the Latin word *constitutio*, establishment).

(1) After independence [from Britain] was proclaimed, every State became a separate nation with its own armed forces, finances, and customs boundaries. These almost independent States [during the period of the Articles of Confederation] sent their representatives to a Congress that had little power.

(2) Although the central power was strengthened under the 1787 Constitution, the States retained considerable independence in local affairs.

(3) A President, elected for four years, becomes the chief executive authority in the country, commanding the army and navy, running the government, and appointing officials. In short, he has enormous authority. George Washington was elected the first President.

(4) The American parliament, called Congress, enacts laws which are subject to approval by the President. Congress consists of two houses. Deputies are elected to the lower house, the House of Representatives, according to the number of people in each State. The upper house of Congress, the Senate, consists of two representatives from each of the States.

(5) The American Constitution reinforced the domination of the large bourgeoisie class (capitalists, merchants, businessmen) and slaveholders. A number of the basic principles of the new American Constitution, as well as

[Continued on next page.]

© 1990 *MIDWEST PUBLICATIONS, P.O. Box 448, Pacific Grove, CA 93950*

Viewpoint B

[Continued from previous page.]

of the State constitutions, were manifestly (obviously) aimed against the masses of people. In almost all the States, one had to have property, either land or capital, in order to vote. Women, slaves, and Indians did not have the right to vote.

(6) In 1791 the United States Constitution was supplemented (added to) by the Bill of Rights. This recognized the citizens' rights to freedom of assembly, freedom of speech, and freedom of conscience; that is, the freedom to profess any religion or to renounce religion altogether. Arbitrary arrests without court order were forbidden.

(7) These "freedoms" exist even now on paper, but they are constantly violated. The Supreme Court, consisting of members appointed for life, was given large authority. This court could void any American law by declaring it unconstitutional. The United States Supreme Court repeatedly supported the slaveholders and bourgeoisie in their struggle against the popular masses. With the help of the Court's decisions, American capitalists frequently succeeded in having worker strikes declared illegal. They dealt harshly with the revolutionary workers. Land that had previously belonged to the Indians was declared the property of the new States and put up for sale.

(8) So-called "bourgeois democracy" was established in North America under the name "popular sovereignty" (democracy), but it was actually the rule of the bourgeoisie.

(9) Nevertheless, the War of Independence did advance development of the United States. The former English colonies became a republic, and England was no longer able to hold back the development of American trade and industry. Customs (trade) taxes were abolished among the former colonies, now States, accelerating the development of trade relations. But slavery, preserved throughout the South, subsequently—almost 100 years later—brought the United States to a new revolution—a civil war; a war between the North and the South.

[Continued on next page.]

Evaluating Foreign Views

1. What can you tell about the situation, beliefs, goals, or concerns of the country in which Viewpoint A was written? What makes you think so?

2. In what country do you think Viewpoint A was written? Why do you think so?

3. What can you tell about the situation, beliefs, goals, or concerns of the country in which Viewpoint B was written? What makes you think so?

4. In what country do you think Viewpoint B was written? Why do you think so?

5. Name two points mentioned in Viewpoint B that surprised you. Why do you think those points were mentioned or emphasized?

LESSON 27   Evaluating Hypothetical Constitutions

Imagine that a constitution has been written for each hypothetical country below. Read the description of each country and, in the space provided, write what chance you think that country's constitution would have of being successful. Explain each of your answers.

Country A

Last year military leaders in Country A assassinated the dictator, who had ruled for the previous seventeen years, and killed 5,000 government workers. The new government, like the old one, uses secret police to keep order. These police kidnap and execute those who oppose the government.

Wealth coming into the country from the sale of oil has created a large middle class. With all its wealth, the government has been able to provide more services, such as free medical care, to all citizens.

Six months ago the military leaders decided that Country A needed a constitution. A five-man committee, appointed by the head military leader, wrote the constitution, which was then ratified (approved) by all thirty members of the legislature. The new constitution stresses the goals of the government, which are to improve the economic conditions of the people, to protect individual liberties, and to provide military security.

Country B

The moderate party gained a majority of seats in the legislature in a recent election and took governmental control from the socialist party which had been in power for two years. Before that time the country had been ruled by dictators.

The country is located in a war-torn region of the world. A revolution is raging in one bordering country, and another country seems to be building up its military to attack Country B.

Country B consists of ten states, each with its own distinct culture (way of life). Most of the people think of themselves as citizens of their individual state, not of the country. There is little thought of helping or dying for one's country.

[Continued on next page.]

Country B

[Continued from previous page.]

When they gained control of the government, the moderate party called for a new constitution to make the country's rules fairer. This constitution, written by delegates chosen by the people, stresses that the government must respect the rights of individual citizens. The constitution can be amended or changed by a majority vote of the legislature. The country's citizens, most of whom are poor and illiterate, ratified the constitution by direct vote, 61% to 39%.

Country C

Two years ago, after gaining independence from a major power, Country C held an election which gave the moderate and pro-military parties the largest number of representatives in its legislature. Since neither party alone had enough representatives to control the government, they agreed to cooperate and to run the government together.

The two parties set up a commission to write a new constitution. These commissioners wrote a constitution, not according to theories of good government, but rather according to practical considerations of what would work for Country C. The constitution protects the political rights of citizens and describes the goals of the government. A "yes" vote by every state within the country is necessary to amend the constitution. It was approved by 75% of the voter-elected delegates to a constitutional convention.

Most people in Country C are extremely poor, among the poorest in the world, with a small minority of the population controlling almost all the wealth. Of those poor citizens who do have jobs, most work for very low wages on the plantations or in the mines and businesses of the rich.

The people love their newly independent country. They sing their national anthem and salute their flag often, and they would be willing to die for their country. In fact, there is widespread opinion within the pro-military party that the country should attack and take over several neighboring countries.

[Continued on next page.]

Country D

This country has a great deal of malnutrition and grinding poverty, with 80–85% of the people illiterate. The country contains fourteen distinct culture groups, twenty different languages, and five major religions.

Perhaps as many as 400,000 people were killed in a recent civil war in which the socialists overthrew the pro-rich party. Now the socialists want to take the land away from the rich and divide it among the poor who have no land.

The constitution was written by twenty-five delegates elected by the people. It establishes a system of checks and balances to control the government's power, guarantees the political and economic rights of all citizens, and states that the goals of the government are to protect the life, liberty, and pursuit of happiness of every citizen. The constitution can be amended by a two-thirds vote of the legislature and a majority vote in three-fourths of the states.

Country E

The abundant land available in this country makes it easy for people to start their own farms and acquire wealth; economic opportunity is available in all kinds of businesses. As a result, most people are middle class, with very few who are poor or feel oppressed by wealthier people. A vast majority of the adults can read, and almost all speak the same language.

Country E has a long tradition of representative government and written laws which everyone, even government officials, must obey. The economy is growing and unemployment is low. Recently, however, a common belief that the old constitution is too weak has arisen among all groups. The people have felt a need to unify the country under a new constitution.

As a result of this, the government has rewritten the constitution. It was written and approved by the wealthier people in society, many of whom are

[Continued on next page.]

Country E

[Continued from previous page.]

well-respected for their fine leadership. The constitution spells out what the government can do, but lists no citizens' rights. Many of the governmental leaders are to be chosen by the representatives of the people, not by the people themselves. There are no provisions for amending the constitution.

Country F

Twenty years ago a group of revolutionaries in Country F overthrew the king and set up a new system intended to improve the economic life of the people. The government took over all the businesses, so now everyone works for the government. This powerful nation has a strong and stable economy. Most people are in the middle class, and almost everyone can read and write.

For the past twenty years, the people have voted in elections in which the candidates have been selected by the ruling party. People who speak out against the government sometimes disappear, never to be heard from again. Nevertheless, many people complain to their friends about the government and its leaders, who they are sure are corrupt.

The constitution, written by government leaders this year, limits government power through division of responsibilities among three branches. It also guarantees protection of individual liberties through courts specifically charged to prevent government violation of rights. The legislature overwhelmingly ratified the constitution, which can be amended only by a three-fourths vote of the legislature.

[Continued on next page.]

 © 1990 MIDWEST PUBLICATIONS, P.O. Box 448, Pacific Grove, CA 93950

Analyzing Factors that Contribute to Successful Constitutions

 Based on your answers for each country, write a paragraph explaining your thoughts on each of the following.

1. What are the two most important factors that contribute to the success of a constitution? Why are they important?

2. What two factors do you consider least important to success of a constitution? Why are they not important?

3. Suppose that these were real countries and that, on the basis of these six countries, someone said, "The key to the success of any country's constitution is a large middle class." Evaluate that claim.

 If, ten years from now, you found out the following information about each of the countries, would you alter your predictions about the success of any of the various constitutions? If so, how and why would it change them?

4.

Country	Situation Ten Years Later
A	New military leaders with different goals are now in power.
B	The neighboring country attacked three years ago, and war is still going on.
C	The liberal party defeated the moderate and pro-military parties in an election two years ago. The liberals have worked within the constitution. They have also pledged to end the war started four years ago when the country attacked two neighboring countries, but, thus far, have been unable to bring about a peaceful settlement.
D	The rich resisted the takeover of their land, so fighting broke out again between government forces and the rich.
E	The people who organized and wrote the constitution formed a political party. This party won the first two elections, but last year the opposition party won and took over the government.
F	The same government is in power, but its goals have changed quite a bit. The economy is still doing well.

[Continued on next page.]

[Continued from previous page.]

 Based on your answers and findings so far, write your reactions to each of the following statements.

5. "A constitution can't create a stable society. Stable societies allow constitutions to work."

6. "The Constitution of the United States was successful because the men who wrote it were practical, not dreamers. They based the new government on experience, not abstract theories."

7. "The key to successful constitutions is compromise. In my country, everyone blames everyone else and won't compromise. The result is violence and the economy is ruined. My country has had a new constitution with each of the past forty-seven presidents, and it won't have a successful constitution until people of all parties are willing to compromise."

8. "The key to the success of the United States Constitution was the tradition of constitutional government already established in the English Colonies. Massachusetts, for example, had had a written constitution since 1629. All the Constitution of 1787 did was ratify the respect for law and order already in existence in the United States."

9. "The key to democratic government, including respect for a constitution, is stable, democratic families. When you have unstable families, you get children who are unrestrained by rules; families dominated by authoritarian fathers result in women and children who are forced to obey unfair, arbitrary rules. How can people be expected to respect the rules of their government when they do not respect the rules made in their own household—or when they have no rules at home?"

10. "People in poor countries today should write constitutions patterned after the United States Constitution of 1787. Then they could establish a democratic system of government based on checks and balances and individual rights."

[Continued on next page.]

[Continued from previous page.]

11. "Given the conditions in the United States in the late 1700s, it would have been hard for the Constitution of 1787 to fail."

12. "The key to the success of any democracy is capitalism. Only when people own their own property do they have real freedom. When the government controls your property it can easily crush your other liberties."

13. "The key to the success of a constitution is a common culture. Multiple cultures are barriers to true nationhood, and without a unified nation a constitution can't survive."

Q Select and study the constitution of any country. You can choose the constitution of any current or historical government.

14. How successful has this constitution been in surviving or in actually establishing a democratic government? Does this constitution tend to support or weaken the criteria discussed above for a successful constitution?

Q Based on what you have read, do you think the following statement is true? If so, why do you think such a condition happens? If not, why not?

15. "A higher percentage of countries today have written constitutions than in the past, but fewer people enjoy real freedom."

[Continued on next page.]

Evaluating Chances for Success

Read the following background information carefully, then create an argument stating how successful you think the new constitution will be. Defend your conclusions with specific reasons.

(1) In 1986 a new president was elected to office in this nation of two thousand islands. The previous president, who has been charged with fraud and with violence during the recent election, resigned and left the country. He had controlled the country for nearly two decades. Democratic government had come to a halt when he declared martial law in 1972, making the army a powerful political force.

(2) As a result of the old government's corruption, the nation's economy was, and remains, in a shambles. During the previous ten years, the islands had gone from one of the wealthiest countries in the region to one of the poorest. The Gross National Product (GNP) has declined for the past two years; the per capita (each person's personal yearly income) is less than $750; there is a large government budget deficit; exports are declining; inflation is very high; 60% of the work force is unemployed or underemployed (working at jobs beneath their skill level for very little pay or not employed full-time throughout the year).

(3) The newly-elected president is an extremely popular leader, and many of the islands' citizens see the current government as the great hope for a return to representation. The new government recently passed a constitution that created a limited representative government; protection of individual rights; and reform of the economy, including help for the poor and land reform to give land to the landless. This constitution was ratified by a majority of the voters.

(4) The new president, however, faces a number of problems. In addition to the economic ills, the government must deal with a communist insurgency. The military, although supportive thus far, is encouraging strong government and military action to crush the rebellion.

LESSON 28   Evaluating Arguments About the Constitution

Q Suppose someone claimed that most Americans supported the Constitution during the period 1787–1789. In the space provided explain how well each of the following would support that claim.

1. The Constitution was approved by a majority of delegates to Constitutional conventions in all twelve states that voted on the Constitution in this time period. The delegates to the state conventions were selected by any adult, free, male citizen (excluding idiots and insane) in some states; other states added property qualifications.

2. The Constitution was written between May 25 and September 17, 1787, by fifty-five delegates to the Constitutional Convention. These men were chosen by their state legislatures.

Q Women were not allowed to vote on delegates to the ratifying conventions. Evaluate the following argument for not allowing women to vote.

3. Men who own no property are dependent on their landlords or employers for survival. Thus, propertyless men can be pressured to vote however the landlords or employers want them to vote. In this way the rich get multiple votes. In the same way, husbands would get two votes if their wives could also vote. It follows that women should not be allowed to vote.

Q Create your own argument on the following situation.

4. The controversy over who was allowed to vote for Constitutional Convention delegates raises the question of who should be allowed to vote in general. Who, if anyone, do you think should be restricted from voting and why?

LESSON 29   Constitutional Conflict:
The Bill of Rights and Freedom of Speech

The Bill of Rights, the first ten amendments to the Constitution, protects the rights of individuals—but only to the extent that they do not conflict with the rights of others. The Supreme Court is the part of the government that decides the meaning and extent of the Bill of Rights in individual cases. In its decisions the Supreme Court follows the idea of *precedent*, that is, that decisions in previous cases set the guidelines for later, similar cases. There must be a very good reason for overturning a precedent set in a previous case. Imagine that you are a Justice of the Supreme Court, and each of the following cases has been appealed to you for decision. Decide each case before going on to the next one.

Concerning freedom of speech, the First Amendment to the U. S. Constitution says: "Congress shall make no law...abridging (reducing) the freedom of speech."

---

1 The Schenck Case

On April 6, 1917, the United States declared war on Germany and entered World War I. A few weeks later Congress passed a draft law, which required men to serve in the military. Later, in 1917 and 1918, Congress passed two Espionage Acts which made it illegal to "attempt to cause insubordination, disloyalty, mutiny or refusal of duty, in the military or naval forces of the United States" and which also made it a crime to "willfully obstruct or attempt to obstruct the recruiting or enlistment service (draft) of the United States," or to write any disloyal language about the United States government.

One of these arrested under the Espionage Acts was Charles T. Schenck, general secretary of the American Socialist Party. Schenck admitted that he printed about 15,000 antidraft leaflets and distributed them to drafted men.

The leaflets referred to the draft as a kind of "slavery," which meant it violated the Thirteenth Amendment to the Constitution. Furthermore, it claimed, the draft helped keep the war going so businessmen could make more money. Since the Constitution did not allow the government to force citizens to fight in a war on foreign soil, the leaflet concluded, drafted men should assert their opposition to the draft.

Schenck, convicted of violating the Espionage Acts, appealed his conviction to the Supreme Court, arguing that everything he printed and said is protected by the First Amendment.

 Should Schenck's conviction be upheld, thereby finding him guilty, or do the Espionage Acts violate his freedom of speech? Explain your decision.

[Continued on next page.]

[Continued from previous page.]

2   The Abrams Case

Jacob Abrams and four other defendants, all immigrants from Russia, were convicted during World War I of violating (breaking) the Espionage Acts. The five printed and distributed leaflets on August 22, 1918, to protest the United States's sending troops into Russia (the USSR). These troops were sent, although the United States was at war with Germany, not Russia, because the government opposed the Communist Revolution which had occurred in Russia.

The leaflet referred to "his Majesty, Mr. Wilson" as a hypocrite for sending American troops to the USSR. It specifically addressed Russian immigrants working in U.S. ammunition factories, saying, "You are producing bullets, bayonets, cannons, to murder not only the Germans, but also your dearest, best, who are in Russia and are fighting for freedom." The leaflet called for a general revolt against the U.S. government.

 Should Abrams's conviction under the Espionage Acts be upheld or do the Espionage Acts violate his freedom of speech? Explain your decision.

3   The Gitlow Case

The State of New York arrested, tried, and convicted Benjamin Gitlow under its criminal anarchy law. This law made it a crime to advocate, advise, or teach forceful or violent overthrow of the government. In June 1919, after World War I, Gitlow, a leader of the American Communist Party, wrote, published, and distributed 16,000 copies of the "Left Wing Manifesto."

This publication called for industrial disturbances, mass strikes, and revolutionary mass action to overthrow and destroy organized parliamentary (representative) government. It concludes with the words, "The Communist International calls the proletariat (workers) of the world to the final struggle!" There was no evidence of any effect resulting from the publication.

 Should Gitlow's conviction under the criminal anarchy law be upheld, or does the law violate his right to free speech? Explain your decision.

[Continued on next page.]

[Continued from previous page.]

4   The Terminiello Case

A few years after World War II, Arthur Terminiello made a speech at a meeting in a Chicago auditorium. The meeting commanded (received) considerable public attention, and the auditorium was filled to its capacity of eight hundred—with another thousand gathered outside to protest the meeting.

In his speech Terminiello made insulting remarks about Jewish people and negative comments about blacks. People in and outside the auditorium were outraged and started yelling and screaming. Terminiello called the people "scum." Those outside began throwing bricks and rocks through the windows of the auditorium.

Mr. Terminiello was arrested, convicted of disorderly conduct in violation of a Chicago city ordinance (law), and fined. The ordinance prohibited people from "making any improper noise, riot, disturbance, [or] breach of the peace...."

 Should Terminiello's conviction under the city's disorderly-conduct ordinance be upheld, or does the law violate his right to free speech? Explain your decision.

5   The Tinker Case

In 1965 a group of adults and students in Des Moines, Iowa, planned to protest the Vietnam War by wearing black armbands to school. On learning of the plan, the principals of the district public schools made a rule to forbid the wearing of armbands. Mary Beth Tinker and two other students wore black armbands to school, refused to remove them, and were suspended until they returned without them.

School officials said they suspended the three students because they feared that the armbands would lead to disturbances and would divert (take) students' attention from their schoolwork. The schools had previously allowed students to wear campaign buttons and other political symbols to school.

 Should the suspension of the three students be upheld, or does the right to free speech protect this type of symbolic protest against such government actions as that in Vietnam? Explain your decision.

MAJOR SOURCES USED FOR LESSONS

Lesson 7

Quinn, David Beers. *Set Fair for Roanoke: Voyages and Colonies, 1584–1606*. Chapel Hill, NC: University of North Carolina Press, 1985.

Sobell, Robert, et al. "Close Up: The Lost Colony of Roanoke." In *The Challenge of Freedom*, 73–8. River Forest, IL: Laidlaw, 1982.

Lesson 8

Fishwick, Marshall. "Was John Smith a Liar?" *American Heritage* 9, no. 6 (October 1958): 28–33+.

Gardner, William E., Robert Beary, and James Olson. "John Smith: History or Hoax?" In *Selected Case Studies in American History*. Vol. 1. Boston: Allyn and Bacon, 1975.

Lesson 9

Carr, Lois Green, and Lorena S. Walsh. "The Planter's Wife: The Experience of Women in Seventeenth-century Maryland." In *The American Family in Social-historical Perspective*, edited by Michael Gordon, 2d ed., 263–88. New York: St. Martin's Press, 1978.

Lesson 10

Boyer, Paul, and Stephen Nissenbaum. *Salem Possessed: The Social Origins of Witchcraft*. Cambridge, MA: Harvard University Press, 1974.

Calef, Robert. "More Wonders of the Invisible World, 1697." Reprinted in *Narratives of the Witchcraft Cases*, edited by G.L. Burr, 289–93. 1914. Reprint. New York: Charles Scribners, 1975.

Caporael, Linda. "Ergotism: The Satan Leashed in Salem?" *Science* 192 (1976): 21–6.

Davidson, James, and Mark Lytle. "The Visible and Invisible Worlds of Salem." In *After the Fact: The Art of Historical Detection*, 28–53. New York: Knopf, 1982.

Hansen, Chadwick. *Witchcraft at Salem*. New York: New American Library, 1969.

Matossian, Mary K. "Ergot and the Salem Witch Affair." *American Scientist* 70, no. 4 (July–August, 1982): 355–7.

Nevins, Winfield. *Witchcraft in Salem Village in 1692*. Salem: The Salem Press, 1916.

Starkey, Marion. *The Devil in Massachusetts*. New York: Doubleday, 1969.

Lesson 15

Bailyn, Bernard. *The Ideological Origins of the American Revolution*. Cambridge, MA: Harvard University Press, 1967.

Gipson, Lawrence Henry. "The American Revolution as an Aftermath of the Great War for the Empire, 1754–1763." *Political Science Quarterly* 65, no. 1 (March 1950): 96–104.

Hacker, Louis. *The Triumph of American Capitalism*. 145–67. New York: Simon and Schuster, 1940.

Lesson 16

Cummins, D. Duane, and William White. *The American Revolution*. Chapters 1–2. Beverly Hills, CA: Benziger, 1973.

Knollenberg, Bernhard. *The Origins of the American Revolution: 1759–1776*. New York: Macmillan, 1960 (Out of Print).

Morgan, Edmund S. and Helen M. Morgan. *The Stamp Act Crisis: Prologue to Revolution*. New York: Macmillan, 1963.

[Continued on next page.]

Lesson 17

Bennett, Peter. *What Happened at Lexington Green?* Menlo Park, CA: Addison-Wesley, 1970.

Force, Peter, ed. *American Archives*. 4th series, 2. Washington, D.C.: Clarke and Force, 1839.

Lesson 21

Feer, Robert A. "Shays's Rebellion and the Constitution: A Study in Causation." *The New England Quarterly* (September 1969): 388–410.

Lesson 23

Ketcham, Ralph, ed. *The Anti-Federalist Papers and the Constitutional Convention Debates*. New York: New American Library, 1986.

Rossitor, Clinton, ed. *The Federalist Papers*. New York: Mentor Books, 1961.

Lesson 25

Beard, Charles. *An Economic Interpretation of the Constitution of the United States*. New York: Macmillan, 1962.

Brown, Robert. "Charles Beard and the Constitution: A Critical Analysis." In *Points of View: Readings in American Government and Politics*, edited by Robert E. DiClerico and Allan Hammock, 44–9. New York: Random House, 1986.

McDonald, Forrest. *We the People: The Economic Origins of the Constitution*. Chicago: University of Chicago Press, 1958.

Lesson 26

U.S. Office of Education. *The American Revolution: Selections from Secondary School History Books of Other Nations*. Washington, D.C.: Government Printing Office, 1976 (Out of Print).

"Selections on the Constitution from Secondary History Books of Other Nations." *This Constitution* 11 (Summer 1986): 32, 37.

Lesson 27

Blondel, Jean. "Constitutionalism and the Role of Constitutions in the Governmental Process." Chap. 15 in *An Introduction to Comparative Government*. New York: Praeger, 1969.

Boston Forum on Global Understanding. "After the Revolution." March 18, 1987. (People from four countries—United States, Mexico, Haiti, and the Philippines—talked about the successes and failures of constitutions in their countries.)

Lesson 29

The Constitutional Rights Foundation. "'Clear and Present Danger' at Home During World War I." *Bill of Rights in Action* 4, no. 3 (Winter 1988): 5–7.

Freund, Paul, et. al. *Constitutional Law: Cases and Other Problems*. Vol 2. Boston: Little Brown, 1967.

Levy, Leonard, Kenneth Karst, and Dennis Mahoney, eds. *Encyclopedia of the American Constitution*. Vols 2 and 4. New York: Macmillan, 1986.